OUT

BOB FIFE
WITH
**RON
HUGHES**

OUT

ONE
CHRISTIAN'S
EXPERIENCE
OF
LEAVING
THE
GAY
COMMUNITY

Kregel
Publications

ISBN 978-0-8254-4440-1

Printed in the United States of America
16 17 18 19 20 21 22 23 24 25 / 5 4 3 2 1

Contents

Introduction

Out traces the story of my life. I am grateful for the nurture and care of friends who have blessed my life and encouraged me to write this book. Looking back, I can see God working to redeem even the most trying and difficult aspects of my life. My own attempts to deal with these often led me into paths of self-indulgence, which I regret. Yet as God restored my relationship with himself, he also began healing broken relationships with others and giving me new, healthy ones that were beyond my deepest longings and wildest dreams. I look forward to what God will do as he continues to work in my life.

Because of the long time period covered in this memoir, I am unable to recall conversations with precision. The dialogue portions of the book have been re-created to convey their sense and intent. Where possible, they have been corroborated by the participants.

I offer this book not as a blueprint for everyone whose life shares some of the same challenges, temptations, or weaknesses as mine, but as a bold declaration that when God is welcomed in, anything can happen. I have seen God work in totally unexpected ways in the lives of those who surrender the broken pieces to him.

Regardless of the specific nature of one's failings, there is hope for new, overflowing, abundant life in relationship with God through the Lord Jesus Christ.

I'd like my story to stand as a testimony to God's unfailing love and grace in the face of sin and rebellion. I trust that it will serve to start conversations and open the hearts of all who read it.

Some may find the account of my early life deeply distressing. Those who prefer to bypass the painful parts of my story may do so at any point by skipping from the end of chapter 1 to chapter 23, entitled "The Story Continues."

1

A Few Hours

The slim young man with short blond hair fit in with the others. Dressed casually in shorts, T-shirt, and sandals, he moved easily through the crowd, scanning those waiting at the rail that separated travelers from their families and friends. I caught his eye, and after exchanging awkward smiles and a quick hug, we headed out of the arrivals lounge at Pearson International Airport. The superficial chatter that characterizes airport conversations kept serious conversation at bay.

We tossed his bags into the trunk and got into the car, where, for the first time since he was a toddler, Sean and I were alone. As we headed downtown, I kept him busy talking about himself, his success at university, his plans, his friends, his mother, and anything I could think of to keep the attention on him—and not just because of my discomfort with what would eventually come up for discussion. I desperately wanted to get back into my boy's life. I'd been even more absent from Sean's life than my father had been from mine.

In spite of the traffic, we reached the apartment before the conversation had truly warmed up. I showed him in and gave him a quick tour. Then I grabbed a couple of soft drinks from the refrigerator and led him to the balcony, where we'd have a view of the sun setting over the city. The air was warm but not stifling, and we settled into our chairs to resume our conversation.

Eventually, Sean turned the spotlight on me, asking about my work, my friends, my life. I couldn't guess what Audrey might or might not have told him about me, so I asked him, "Do you know about me?"

"What are you referring to, Dad?" He turned the question back on me.

"Well, you know that I'm . . ."—the word stuck in my throat—"gay."

"Yeah," he replied, "I know."

"Your mom tell you?"

"Yeah."

"When?" I asked.

"Last week while I was with her in Texas."

"What do you think about that?" I asked.

"Well," he paused for a moment. "I guess if you are, then you are, and that's the way it is."

That bit went better than I'd thought it might. He didn't put me down. He didn't tell me I should try to change. But before I could respond, he continued.

"And Dad, I want you to know . . ."—now he choked on his words— "that my love for you is unconditional."

Well! I couldn't remember the last time I'd heard of "unconditional love." Anything that had passed for love in the last twenty years of my life always came with strings attached, with conditions, with an expiration date. Sean's simple statement cut me deeply. Here was my son, showing real love to me, a man he barely knew. Something about it stirred my memory. He reminded me of another young man who might have done such a thing once. One with a distant father unworthy of his love. Tears brimmed over my eyelids and ran down my face. My father had already passed beyond my reach forever.

Our conversation abated, and only the roar of the traffic below, punctuated by the occasional blast of a horn, broke the silence. Impulsively, before I could stop myself, I blurted out, "Sean, I'm going to tell you something I hadn't planned to say. But as I sit here looking at you and thinking about my own life, I swear that if there's a way out of the life I'm living, and if I can find that way, I want to get out."

What I didn't say was that I honestly didn't think getting out was at all possible because I was enmeshed in everything gay. But here was my son, calling me "Dad" and talking about love. I had to at least make an attempt. I was hungry for reality—for what I had known long ago with my own family and lost completely.

We sat for a while in emotion-laden silence. I wanted to touch him, to put my arm around him, to hug him, but I couldn't. *How would he take it?* I wondered. *Would he think I was coming on to him?* Touching had been a prelude to sex for so long for me that I couldn't imagine anything different. So we sat there—he in his chair, I in mine—mourning the gulf between us and trying to find a way to bridge it.

We'd only been together a few hours, yet we were into one of the most profound conversations of my life. I suggested we go back into the apartment and find something to eat. Sean watched as I prepared pasta sauce from scratch. I avoided using canned sauces; my own sauce, though time consuming to make, was better. We were in no hurry, and meal preparation allowed our conversation to flow naturally into lighter areas.

As I chopped onions, sliced mushrooms and celery, and gathered the spices to add to the tomatoes simmering on the stove, we chatted about cooking, music, and sports, particularly the Blue Jays. Having had so little interaction in the past, what would normally be trivialities came as great revelations. The hundreds of similarities and differences between fathers and sons were laden with significance. Something as simple as sharing a meal of penne in rich tomato sauce with a salad and toasted garlic bread assumed an importance far beyond what anyone could have imagined.

We lingered over the food and, even after it was all gone, sat there chatting as the minutes turned into hours. Eventually our stamina gave way to fatigue and we were ready to call it a day. I wasn't sure how comfortable Sean would be with me, so I decided to let him have the apartment to himself at night. We said our good-nights, and I drove over to the house where I had started to set up my new living space amid the rubble of the past.

I got into bed, and as I lay in the darkness waiting for sleep, I thought about what I'd said to Sean. I couldn't believe my own words. I hadn't intended to say them, but I had to admit to myself I truly wanted to get out of the life I'd been living. I just didn't know if I could. I was in deep. My whole life revolved around gay culture. I couldn't think of a single experience I wanted but hadn't had. My life investments certainly had paid well in short-term dividends that satisfied my immediate desires and stroked my ego. But long term? These few hours with Sean confronted me with a world of good on which I had turned my back. The awareness that I still valued these things hit me like a wild pitch. *I did it once,* I thought. *I left one life for another. I'll do it again.*

Scenes from my past drifted through my mind as the sleepless hours passed.

2

The Mirror

At first the noises were indistinct to my drowsy mind, but a sudden cry of pain snapped me to full consciousness as surely as one of my father's backhanded slaps. My body stiffened with fear as I became aware that my father was beating Mom. The sound of hushed voices, one menacing, one pleading, were punctuated with the sounds of rough hands striking soft flesh.

I'd heard this kind of thing before, but tonight seemed different. The snarling threats were crueler, the stifled cries more intense, the sound of the blows louder. I became convinced my father intended to kill Mom. Already awake, Ronnie rocked quietly in his bed trying to comfort himself. Though eight years older than me, my mentally challenged brother would be no help to me. He feared our father more than I did—and with good reason. Of all the children, he was the only one who might have experienced my father's wrath more than I did. With total disregard for Ronnie's disability, or maybe because of it, my father would brutalize him with words and blows.

I slipped from my bed and silently opened the door to the room shared by my sisters Barb and Gwen. Only two years older, Gwen was closer to me than my other siblings, both chronologically and emotionally. I roused her and she joined me, crouching near the top of the stairs,

13

listening to the sickening sounds coming from our parents' room. She pointed down the stairs, and our bare feet made no sound on the heavy pine boards as we crept down and slipped through what we called "the breakfast room" into the kitchen, where the phone hung on the wall. Gwen suggested we call the police. Shivering with fear, I agreed.

I stood watch by the foot of the stairs to ensure that our father didn't surprise us. When Gwen finished the call, she looked at me in a way that said, "Now we've done it!" I remember how her pigtails jiggled as she trembled. What would come next? Would our father beat us with his horse harness? Would he do something worse? Would the police arrest our father and put him in jail? Would Mom be alright?

The terrifying noises were getting louder. My other sisters would be awake now too, lying still in their beds, praying our father's anger would not spill out of Mom's room to be unleashed on them. Gwen motioned toward the back door. It would be safer outside if things boiled over upstairs. Our shoes and slippers were in our rooms, but we had no intention of returning for them. The heavy door creaked softly as we eased it open on its frozen hinges.

We stood on the concrete slab outside, our feet melting little patches of frost as we shuffled back and forth. In our hurry, we hadn't thought to grab our coats. So there we were, wearing nothing but our pajamas, trying to keep from freezing on this early December night. Still, the fear of what might await us inside kept us from returning to the warmth of the house. To be safe, we'd have to stay where we were until the police arrived.

My father, who had a knack for starting businesses and seducing women, left us in a state of constant tension wondering when he might show up. When I had arrived home after finishing my paper route that evening, I sensed the calm that announced he was distracted elsewhere. His absence was as palpable as his presence.

When present, my father bolstered his sense of authority with belittling comments, slaps, and backhands. Occasionally, when he got extra worked up, he'd come after me with a piece of light horse harness gripped in the cigarette-yellowed fingers of his bulky right hand. His handsome face would be red with rage. His aim was wild as he chased me around the table with his improvised whip, but his strength guaranteed a welt wherever the leather made contact. Sometimes my mother would make me stay home from school for as long as it took the marks to fade.

I had smiled to myself and relaxed when I realized that my father was away. I expected a quiet evening: some supper, a couple hours of listening to the radio or reading a comic book, and then bed. Mom always insisted we get a good sleep on Saturday nights so we could get up early for Sunday school.

Ronnie and I used the wide hallway at the top of the stairs as a bedroom, though it lacked privacy. Gwen and Barb, two and four years older than me, shared one room. Yvonne, ten years my senior, had her own room. Our parents used the third bedroom; since my father spent more time away than at home, I thought of it as "Mom's room." All three bedrooms opened into the hall where Ronnie and I slept, but we were used to living in close quarters and never thought of our setup as unusual. In fact, things had eased considerably since my oldest brother, Ken, left home to join the Canadian military.

The evening had unfolded as anticipated, and Ronnie and I had tucked ourselves in by nine o'clock. Delivering the afternoon papers in the cold, fresh air had left me eager for rest, and I quickly fell asleep. Now, shivering with my sister in cold and fear, I realized that my father had crept up the stairs, his mood as dark as the stairwell, in order to surprise Mom in bed. I wondered what had started his rage, how long he'd been abusing Mom, and what would happen when the police arrived.

Mercifully they came quickly. When we heard the car, we hurried back inside and ran through the house to let them in the front door. We didn't want their knocking to alert my father. The two big officers quietly asked where our parents were. We told them and followed them up the stairs. They approached the door, and one of them raised his hand to knock on it with his knuckles. The sound of a crash and breaking glass from inside the room masked the sound, and the police burst through the door without waiting any longer.

We watched Mom trying to cover herself in the presence of these strange men and my father trying to act nonchalant and belligerent at the same time. Pieces of the big dresser mirror glinted among the odds and ends on the dresser top, stuck out of a half-opened drawer, and lay scattered over the floor. The Vaseline jar that shattered the glass had rolled to a stop near the foot of the bed. We couldn't tell whether my father had intended the mirror as his target or if it merely became collateral damage when my mother dodged the missile.

I had never seen my father play any part but that of absolute authority, so I found this role change strange to witness. The police lectured our father about the legal ramifications of domestic abuse. They assured him they'd not treat him so leniently if they caught him repeating this night's mayhem. My father blustered and groveled by turns, attempting to get them out of the house, but they took their time and made their point.

Until he left again on business, Gwen and I lived in terror of punishment for our intervention, but it never came. It was as if the visit from the police had never happened. To be fair, our father reduced the physical aspect of his abuse of Mom for a while, though the verbal assaults continued.

Whether or not any relationship existed between that night and what happened a few weeks later, we couldn't know. For the first and only time I remember, our father bought us children a big Christmas present: a toboggan large enough for all of us to share.

3

A Family Secret

I patted Tippy's head. The little black-and-white terrier sat by my side as I gazed through the wooden porch railing, watching for Mom. After a few minutes she came out of the grocery store down the street, where she worked. I could tell by the way her steps dragged and her shoulders heaved that she was weeping.

As she drew closer, Tippy and I went out to meet her. She hadn't had her fiftieth birthday, yet with her white hair and wrinkled face, she looked more like my grandmother than my mother. She told people that her hair had started turning when she was in her late teens. For years she wore it pulled back from her face, emphasizing her pronounced nose and coarse features. Mom was of medium height but had a generous bosom, which usually went unnoticed because of her chronically apologetic posture—shoulders rounded, head slightly bowed. On Sundays, though, when she played the piano at church, she liked to wear bright clothes, a string of pearls, and a hat, and in that outfit she stood a little straighter and displayed some inner strength.

On this day, as she walked home from work in her plain print dress, she would have been invisible to me if she hadn't been my mother. When she saw me, she wiped her face with her hand and tried to smile.

"Hi, Mom." I ignored her red eyes. "Tippy and I were waiting for you."

"Have you finished your paper route and done your chores, Bob?" she asked.

"Yes, Mom, all done."

"That's good. You know your father would be angry if he got home and found you playing if there was still work to do." Her voice was tired, but more than that, it was sad.

"Is he coming home tonight?" I asked.

"I don't expect so, but we never know."

"Mom?" I screwed up my courage. "Why are you crying?"

In response, she hurried her steps and covered her face. I jogged to keep up as we turned off the sidewalk at our house and climbed the steps to the long veranda. "What's wrong, Mom? I just wondered."

With her hand on the doorknob, Mom looked down at me. I could see her face wavering between warmth and hardness. "Listen, Bob," she said with steel in her voice. "Today I got my pay. I had to give most of it back to the store to pay for the food we've been eating for the last week. I still have to make payments on the hydro and telephone. Thank God it's warm enough that we don't need to buy oil this time of year. I don't know what's going to happen this winter."

"It won't be winter for a long time, Mom," I reasoned. "You can save some by then."

"Don't be giving me advice about what I should be doing," she snapped. "You're starting to sound like your father."

Her words stung. I'd been trying to understand her sadness and make her feel better, but I had only made things worse, and now I felt bad as well. I knew she didn't like my father and now it sounded like maybe she didn't like me either. I didn't have much time to think about it, though. She opened the door, slipped through, and closed it firmly behind her. I stood staring at the doorknob, wondering whether I should follow her in.

Thinking better of it, I called Tippy, and with the one family member I could always count on, I walked toward the railroad tracks, hoping to find someone to play with. It was late spring and still bright and warm enough, but no one was there. At that hour, most of the moms on our street would be serving the evening meal to their husbands and children. My mom had to work to put food on the table.

I threw sticks for Tippy, but he wasn't in the mood to play. When I threw one, he just lay down and gnawed on it. So I called him and returned home. I entered quietly and heard Mom and my oldest sister, Yvonne, in the kitchen. Yvonne already had a job and was looking for a boy to marry her and take her away. My sisters didn't have the freedom that my oldest brother, Ken, had. The Second World War was over by the time he was old enough to sign up for the army, but he did anyway. Was his motivation purely patriotic or rooted in his desire to get away from home—far away? The regular visits to the paymaster only sweetened the deal for him.

With five of us depending on Mom's salary for food and shelter, meals were always simple but sufficient. We didn't linger long at the table, engaging in warm or stimulating conversation. Mealtime had a specific function—to fill our bellies as efficiently as possible—and once that was realized, we moved on to other necessities. After supper, I went to the breakfast room to read a comic book before going to bed. Yvonne followed me.

"You shouldn't be bothering Mom when she's sad," Yvonne said. "It only makes her feel worse. Mom doesn't earn much money, and Dad won't help her. It's not fair."

"I only wanted to know what was wrong so I could cheer her up." I paused before taking a guess. "Maybe she was thinking about Jack."

Yvonne looked startled. "What do you know about Jack?"

"Not much," I replied. "Only that when they talk about him, our father gets angry and Mom gets sad."

"I guess you should know about him so you don't say the wrong thing sometime and get everyone upset," she said.

At seventeen, Yvonne already knew enough of the ways of the world to empathize with Mom in ways the rest of us couldn't, and she was able to explain things to us that Mom would never talk about. "When Mom was about my age," my sister began, "she fell in love with Jack. She was crazy about him, but Grandma and Grandpa didn't think he was good enough for her. Jack and Mom tried to keep their relationship secret, but they were caught together often enough that Grandpa decided he had to break them up permanently.

"He knew our father was very ambitious and had a good business sense. Grandpa thought that he would be able to give Mom a better life than Jack could. So he told Jack to stay away from Mom and forbade her from ever seeing him again. At the same time, Grandpa and Grandma began inviting our father to their house. He started being friends with Mom. He was very kind to her and cheered her up a little. Once Mom trusted him a bit, he started to take advantage of the situation."

I understood all the words but, at the time, was just beginning to grasp their significance.

"Mom didn't really love him," Yvonne continued, "but he was there. He was friendly. He made her feel good. Even though she was still really in love with Jack, she found herself becoming more involved with Grandpa's choice for her. Before she knew it, a wedding was arranged and she was married to this man who was not her true love.

"As soon as it was too late, she realized that she'd been tricked by our grandfather and father into doing something she regretted. Someday you'll understand what this meant between Mom and Dad as a husband and wife, but she had already given her heart to Jack. Father sensed this. He knew that she didn't really love him and had given something to Jack that he could never have. That hurt his pride. He hated Mom for loving Jack even though she could never have him. He hated Jack for being Mom's true love. Now our father tries to punish her by having other girlfriends, but Mom says she'll stay with him until you're grown up enough."

This isn't good, I thought. *Am I somehow responsible for keeping the family together? When will I be "grown up enough"? What will happen then?*

"Now you know the story and why we must never mention the name

'Jack' around our parents. Mom gets a beating every time our father is reminded of him." She paused to think for a moment and then continued. "And Mom? All she can think about is how much happier she would have been with Jack."

She leaned back and looked deeply into my eyes. "Do you know how important this is, Bob?" she asked.

Wide-eyed at the revelation, I nodded. It explained some things. It also produced a lot of questions, but I sensed that now wasn't the time to ask.

4

Shut Out

Unbidden, a sob sputtered from my lips. Immediately three pairs of eyes swung upward to the grate in the ceiling. I kept still, knowing they couldn't see me above them in the darkness.

"Get back into bed, Bob," Yvonne said from her place at the table behind one of three piles of penny candy, licorice, and chocolate bars. Yvonne, simple in every way, was plump, unambitious, and usually jovial. But she was easily influenced when the sisters were together, and I often served as the outside enemy that bound them together.

"This stuff is just for girls," added Barb with a red Twizzler hanging from her mouth. My middle sister was a big, buxom girl with dark hair cut to a medium length. I'd say she was more attractive than pretty because her warm personality outshone her looks. With everyone else she was friendly and personable, but I was only her irritating little brother—someone to be generally avoided and, when that wasn't possible, pushed to the periphery.

"There's nothing here for you." Gwen delivered the deepest wound of all because of our closeness. Even as an adolescent, Gwen was self-aware and maximized her considerable physical beauty. She was outgoing and attractive, and she carried herself well. From childhood she had always aspired to bigger and better things. One of the ways girls got ahead in those days was through the men they could attract, and Gwen knew how to attract masculine attention. She put a lot of energy into looking good and was always ready for the occasion, whatever it was. A natural leader, Gwen had considerable influence over her older sisters, and I knew she could have changed the tone of the moment. But she hadn't the inclination.

Half an hour earlier, as soon as Mom left to work her second job at the service center, they had sent me off to bed and then slipped out of the house, leaving Ronnie watching *I Love Lucy* on the TV in the breakfast room and me alone upstairs, contemplating the injustice of being banished to my bed.

I could picture everything. The girls would have headed straight to Nelly's Hot Dog Stand—the rendezvous point for all the kids in the neighborhood. The older kids gave most of their attention to each other, flirting and quietly inventing ways to ditch their younger siblings if they could find someone to go with them to the woods by the railway tracks. The younger kids focused on the treats to be had: black balls, bubble gum, licorice and strawberry Twizzlers, caramels, jujubes, and other assorted delights.

I had heard them talk about their trips to Nelly's so often that I could picture the scene. Along with the laughing, joking, and chatting, Gwen and Barb would be manipulating Yvonne into spending money on them. She alone had a full-time job, so she had the most dollars. Luckily for her two younger sisters, she also had the least sense and could usually be convinced to buy them treats.

I didn't have to imagine them at home splitting up the loot. They did it on the table directly under the grate that allowed warm air from the first floor to pass upstairs. As soon as I'd hear them come in, I'd scoot out of bed and lie on the floor with my face pressed against the chilly metal. From my vantage point above, I could watch them eating their goodies and listen to them talking about the other kids they'd seen at Nelly's. Sometimes I'd betray myself with a sound, and immediately, as now, they would turn on me.

Disheartened, I returned to my bed and lay there, tossing. *Why are they so mean? Why don't they share? Maybe they just hate all boys,* I thought, remembering the mayhem of the evening before.

It was Ronnie's turn to do the dishes, and as soon as Mom had gone, Yvonne announced loudly that she wasn't going to let him watch *I Love Lucy.*

He immediately became belligerent. "Why not?" he shouted. "You know I always watch *I Love Lucy.* It's my show. I always, always watch it."

"You can't watch it 'cause we want to watch something else," said Gwen.

"I'm going to watch it and you can't stop me." Anger tinged his voice.

"I'm going to watch it and you can't stop me," parroted Barb in a singsong voice.

Immediately the others joined in. "I'm going to watch it and you can't stop me," they cried over and over, sometimes together, sometimes one by one. Ronnie glared at his tormentors in frustration.

"Don't get mad and hit us or we'll tell Mom and she'll never let you watch *Lucy* again." Yvonne's threat both baited him and expressed fear that his anger would translate into actions.

"I'll hit you if I want and you can't stop me," he shouted.

"I'll hit you if I want and you can't stop me," Barb sang out.

This initiated another round of mockery to fuel his growing rage.

My sisters played this game with Ronnie every so often. They were amused by the intensity of his reaction to being told he couldn't watch *I Love Lucy.* The show meant nothing to them but everything to him, rating as the highlight of his day. Ronnie couldn't imagine anything worse than being deprived of this simple pleasure. To miss it would upset his whole routine.

Last night the girls had gone too far. Their cruelty pushed Ronnie past shouting to lashing out with superhuman strength. If Ronnie ever hit you when he was in a rage, you never let it happen again. Mom feared he'd do some real damage, and she had forbidden the girls from egging him on. But in her absence, sometimes temptation overtook them. I watched in fear as Ronnie flung the tea towel to the floor and charged toward Barb. She screamed and the girls scattered, fleeing out different doors into the safety of the yard. I kept quiet and waited, listening to Ronnie muttering under his breath, grimly warning his absent tormentors that they'd "better not come back in here." He settled down when the *I Love Lucy* theme came on the TV. The girls knew they would have been in real trouble if Ronnie had gotten hold of one of them. Now they'd leave him alone for a few weeks.

I could never understand the girls. One-on-one they could be OK with me, but put them together and something happened. Something bad. They became unkind. I confess I thought of them in fairy-tale terms as the "three ugly stepsisters." While they routinely pushed me away, I just as routinely attempted to have a relationship with them.

As the years passed, the tension between us eased. Yvonne and Barb got married and moved out. Throughout our middle teen years, without our older sisters to shift the balance of social power, Gwen and I became quite good friends. We walked to school together and I became her protector, defending her from the kids she often provoked with her quick wit and sharp tongue.

5

The Soldier's Visit

My eldest brother, Ken, always did his best to avoid our father. I remember his hiding out when he got home from school, waiting until after Father had eaten his supper and left for the evening. I don't know how other people regarded our father, but he left a wake of fear and insecurity as he roared through the lives of his children.

Our father was probably the only person on the planet who intimidated Ken, who was fit, athletic, and always well groomed with his military-style haircut. Along with his strong physical presence, Ken was assertive to the point of being domineering. His regimented, militaristic approach to relationships and family life provoked us to resent him and his overbearing ways. He had opinions about everything and didn't hesitate to express them and make clear his disdain for anyone who didn't share them.

The Canadian military met Ken's needs. It provided a social environment that matched his personal style. It gave him a haven from our father, close fraternal relations in the brotherhood of soldiers, confidence-building physical-fitness training, a clearly defined purpose for his life, and enough money to impress girls. Ken joined the army as I entered first grade, and in so doing, he exited my life for the next forty years.

Mom and Ken shared the bond unique to mother and firstborn son, and when he would get a few days of leave, he'd come home to see her. He timed his visits to suit her schedule; he and I didn't cross paths often. Even as a boy, I could see that after a few years, he had attained his adult size and build and, with them, a heightened level of self-assurance. He displayed a cocky air, especially when in uniform, which gnawed at me like Tippy on a big old hambone.

With a frequently absentee father, another brother with a mental disability, and three older sisters, I cut out a role for myself in the family that this swaggering, big guy in military fatigues threatened. Once he showed up unexpectedly. The girls kowtowed to him as if he were some sort of hero; they admired their brother with his oversized presence and vied for his attention in a way that made me feel even more alienated than usual. I resented his walking in with his take-charge attitude and destabilizing the family hierarchy, or at least my perceived place in it. So when the opportunity came for me to defy one of his "orders," I did. Somebody needed to let him know his rank hadn't changed at home just because he wore a uniform.

Ken wasn't impressed and decided to put me in my place. So there we were in one of the most lopsided matches imaginable: a twenty-two-year-old soldier with four years of military life under his belt having a showdown with his adolescent brother in front of their sisters. With little effort, he threw me onto the couch and held me down. In the process he pushed my face into a pillow. Winded from the altercation, I tried to suck air into my lungs but couldn't. Neither could I cry out. I flailed, fearful of being suffocated, but Ken, not knowing I couldn't breathe, just held me more firmly. Only when I lay still under him did he say, "Don't forget this lesson soon, Bob, or you'll get another one," and let me up.

I felt humiliated, not acknowledging the imbalance in age and development. Unbeknownst to Ken, he had become one more man in my life who might hurt me at will. I couldn't wait for him to get back to his base so what family order we had could be restored.

6

A Hundred-Dollar Thrashing

Among my father's business enterprises was a service center comprised of a gas station and diner on the Belleville highway on the outskirts of Trenton. Mom ran the diner in the evenings after she finished her grocery-store job. Over the years, we kids all had stints there of various lengths, pumping gas or serving food. We were too young for anyone else to hire us, but we were old enough to be useful at the service center, and while our father didn't place much value on education, he did value work.

Among my mother's responsibilities was to buy supplies for the diner. She was usually quite organized about this and did all of the shopping for the week at one time, but it was impossible to always estimate demand accurately. On occasions when she ran short of small items like coffee or cream, she'd tell my father, and he'd give her money to pick them up at the grocery store where she worked during the days.

One day on my way home from school, my buddies were talking about going to Nelly's Hot Dog Stand to buy some treats. I didn't have any money, but I remembered seeing a stack of coins on the table that morning and thought I'd grab a few so I could feel like one of the guys with a few cents to spend. I asked them to wait for me and dashed into the house. Sure enough, the coins were there on the table. I picked a couple off the top and ran back to join them. When I got to the hot-dog stand, I discovered I had a quarter and a nickel. I spent it all on potato chips and penny candy. I had enough that I even shared with one of the guys who only had a dime.

I enjoyed the feeling of connectedness with the fellows as we walked back down the street eating our treats, joking and talking about the day's ordinary, humorous events: someone's ripped pants, a girl's embarrassment, a teacher's misspelled word on the blackboard.

I got home just in time for supper only to find that my father was joining us. He had added some weight to his once fit frame and started to lose his hair. Conversation between my parents came in snippets of information about the details of the day. We children were not encouraged to talk about our lives, since our father didn't find them particularly interesting.

It was my turn to do dishes so, after we'd finished eating, my sisters cleared the table and I went to the kitchen to get on with the job while Yvonne served coffee to my parents in the living room. I was barely aware of what they were talking about with the clattering of the dishes, yet somehow I picked out some of Mom's words: "Cliff, you left money for me to pick up coffee today, but it was thirty cents short. Can you give that to me now so I can pick up a can at the store on my way to the diner this evening?"

I froze. I knew why she was thirty cents short. This would not be good.

My father asked no questions. I knew what lay ahead when I heard him snarl, "I'll get him." There was no cover in the kitchen. I ran to the dining room, arriving just before he did. The large, heavy dining table was all that stood between us, and as he wrapped his leather strap around his fist, he started after me. I scrambled to keep out of his reach as he began swinging. He was in no hurry; he knew he'd get me sooner or later.

Whenever the lash landed on my body, I'd cry out, as much in fear as in pain. After he hit me half a dozen times, I was sobbing. Mom came into the room and tried to intervene. He pushed her aside roughly and she toppled into a dining-room chair.

"Cliff, that's enough." Her voice was shrill with tension.

"Shut up, Edith." His voice was cold. "He'll get what's coming to him. I'm not raising a thief. I'll whip it out of him."

Over and over he struck me. He was cool and methodical. Most of my back and legs were throbbing by the time his rage started to subside. I knew I'd miss some school over this. Finally he landed a particularly heavy blow to my lower back, and I collapsed on the floor. He stood over me threatening me with something far worse if I took so much as a penny from him again. When the emotional pummeling reached the level of the physical beating, he reached into his pocket for a few coins, threw them into Mom's apron, and strode out of the house.

Mom picked me up. We were both crying as she led me upstairs to my bed. She seldom comforted me physically, but she did that night, though only for a few minutes. "I've got to go, Bob," she whispered. "I've got to pick up that can of coffee and get to the diner."

She rose and untied her apron; then, rolling it into a ball around her hand, she stepped to the top of the stairs. "Bob, you just got a hundred-dollar thrashing for the thirty cents you took. Promise me you'll never steal money again."

I nodded, sobbing. I wasn't sure I'd never steal again, but I was sure that if I ever did, I'd do a lot better job of not getting caught.

Her good-night faded as she disappeared down the stairs. I heard the door close behind her.

7

Hijinks

In spite of the troubles at home, I enjoyed a largely carefree childhood. I lived on the undisciplined edge of life along with my best friends, Danny and Carl. They were the leaders of the boys our age, and while I wasn't a tough kid, I admired these guys, who seemed fearless not only of their peers but of authority as well.

I didn't excel as a student. Unmotivated and undisciplined, I couldn't even bother being intentionally rebellious. I routinely got into low-level trouble for failing to do my homework, going off school property during the day, and being uncooperative with the teachers. Mr. Harris once got so frustrated with the class that he threatened to give the next person who turned around a strapping. His words passed in but then out of my memory, and he seemed particularly glad that I was the one he caught. Hauling me from my seat to the front of the class, he administered several strokes on each hand. I didn't give him the satisfaction of crying in front of my classmates, though my hands were red and smarting. He couldn't bear my unrepentant attitude and sent me to the principal's office. Mr. Martin was a burly fellow and took on the challenge of breaking me. Sitting in his big chair, he took my wrist in his left hand and raised the strap high with his right. Instinctively, just as the strap was about to smack my already sore palm, I curled my fingers into a fist and jerked my hand back to avoid the blow. That left Mr. Martin's own leg to absorb the strap's momentum.

Mr. Martin now took a personal interest in the proceedings. I was sobbing before I left his office, but I pulled myself together on the way back to class, and at recess I impressed my friends with my puffy red hands and my account of how the principal had strapped himself before he strapped me. This event, and others like it, convinced me that the best thing about school was social interaction with my buddies.

One spring day Carl brought a hook and line with him to school and managed to catch an eel out of the Trent River just as the bulk of the kids were on their way past. When he spotted me, he waved me over and showed me the ugly beast. Malevolent excitement gripped him. "Let's wait for a bunch of girls and chase them with it." I quickly agreed, and since I had a better reputation, I agreed to lure the girls as close as I could before he'd jump up and chase them.

Within a minute or two half a dozen girls, some from our class and some younger, approached the bridge. "Hey girls," I called, "come here for a minute. Look at this. Carl wonders if he should take it in for show-and-tell."

That piqued their curiosity, and while two hung back, justifiably suspicious, four of them walked over to us. Carl crouched with one knee on the ground, keeping the writhing creature out of sight, while I stood in front of him blocking the view. As soon as I thought they were close enough for him to catch, I stepped to one side, cueing Carl to leap to his feet and begin the chase.

He launched himself toward them shouting, "First one I catch gets this down her back."

They let out a volley of screams and, with adrenaline fueling their skinny schoolgirl legs, ran as hard as they could toward safety. Carl only chased them for twenty paces or so and then stopped, unable to run farther because he was laughing so hard. He called after them, "I'm going to get you," eliciting another round of verbal hysterics. The two of us stood by the bridge, laughing and bragging to Danny and another friend who had just arrived.

Carl threw the eel back into the river and we continued toward school, enjoying the hilarity known only to boys on the cusp of adolescence. We found girls to be very interesting creatures but had yet to discover a way to draw out an intense reaction from them other than by frightening or threatening them. But while girls were fun to tease and terrorize, we boys found true fellowship only in each other's company. Together we had a sense of belonging, adventure, and invincibility.

During the summer we had lots of time to engage in risky behavior. Some things, like skinny-dipping in the deep hole up the river, weren't really dangerous, just exciting—especially considering the possibility of someone, maybe even a girl, catching us in the water and stealing our clothes. No one ever did, but that didn't lessen the shame potential—or the thrill.

One game we played was substantially more dangerous. A high railway trestle crossed the Trent River just outside of town. We'd climb up on it, meters above the water, put small objects on the tracks, and watch what happened when the train passed over them. We didn't take chances with the fast-moving passenger trains, but the slow freights begged for our attention. Sometimes we'd play hobo, jumping onto a car and then hanging on for dear life as the train made its way down a spur to the creosote plant, where it would stop to pick up a load of railway ties. No one ever got hurt, and we never got caught by the local police, the railway cops, or our parents. Playing on and around the trains momentarily satisfied our appetite for thrills.

Within our group of peers of about eight boys, we had all managed to acquire BB guns. With these weapons, we raised the stakes of our games of war and of cops and robbers. We would meet at the woods by the railway tracks, divide into teams, and scatter to hunt each other down. We were not entirely bereft of mental faculties and frequently rehearsed the one big rule: "Always aim at the other guy's legs." We all knew that if anyone ended up with a mark on his face or, worse yet, an eye injury, there would be big trouble for all of us.

On one occasion, we were playing cops and robbers in the woods by the railway tracks when someone got a little excited and raised his gun too high. Carl took a BB on his shoulder. Stung, he threw down his gun and started yelling. We gathered around him while he lectured and threatened the "cops." The game was spoiled for that day. We all realized the miscalculation could have ended in tragedy. But the afternoon had barely begun, so Danny suggested a change. Keeping the same teams, we'd hunt birds. First team to bring a dead bird back to the old tree the "robbers" used as their hideout would be the winners.

This was safer for us boys, to be sure, and not gravely dangerous for the birds. None of us were snipers, and since our weapons had a muzzle velocity barely surpassing a peashooter, even a direct hit was likelier to bounce off the feathers than penetrate. The robbers under Carl's leadership fanned out to the west. Those of us who had been cops under Danny spread out heading east. I hadn't gone far when I heard the sound of a woodpecker. His steady *tap-tap-tap* drew me to him for our encounter with destiny.

He was a small bird. I knew nothing about him other than that he fell into the woodpecker category and was concentrating hard on his work. I approached him from behind so he couldn't see me. Then, when I was close enough that I thought I could hit him, I sidled my way around to the right. I knew if I didn't hit him in the head, my BB would do nothing but scare him away to another tree. Leaning on a big old maple for support, I slowly raised my gun.

I forced myself to breathe slowly and quietly. My hands were trembling. I'd never made a serious attempt on a life before. Three times I drew a bead on his eye, and three times my hands quivered so that I had to start over before I could squeeze the trigger. On my fourth attempt I was ready. As soon as I had a line between the sights and his eye, I'd shoot; that way I wouldn't have to try to hold my aim. I started just below him and slowly brought the muzzle of the gun up while I stared down the barrel. As soon as I saw his eye, I squeezed my hand. The little rifle gave its characteristic *phut!* and the woodpecker dropped to the bottom of the tree, where it lay twitching.

I ran up and stared at my victim. Mostly by luck, I had hit him just behind his eye. The BB hadn't had enough force to penetrate his little skull, but it had certainly hit him harder than anything had ever hit him before. I hoped he'd get to his feet—a little stunned, perhaps, and with a big headache for sure, but otherwise OK—and, with a hop, take to the air and hide from me. But as I watched, the twitching grew feebler and eventually stopped. I was a killer.

I didn't know what to do. I wanted to be the hero to my friends, but I felt anything but heroic. I'd never touched anything dead before; I pulled a leaf from a handy maple sapling and, using it to shield my hand from contact with the corpse, I picked up the woodpecker by one leg. After a few steps, I felt a modicum of courage return, and I began calling to my buddies, telling them the game was over and I was the winner.

I got back to the tree first and laid the victim on a small, smooth stone. The boys returned, oohing and clucking in admiration of my hunting prowess. I wouldn't let anyone touch the bird or poke him with sticks as some wanted to do. I'd killed him; the least I could do was protect his dignity. After all of the boys had returned and I was acknowledged as having won the day for the cops, Carl asked me what I was going to do with him.

"I'm going to bury him," I said.

Carl said it would be easier to throw him into the bushes and let a fox eat him. I was adamant. So Danny suggested that, now that the fun was over, they should leave me alone to do my grave digging. As I scratched away the forest litter with a sharp stick and dug a little hole, the others left.

When the hole was about eight inches deep, I dropped the bird in it, covered him with the leaf, filled in the hole, and then topped it with the stone I had laid him on, pressing it level with the dirt. I finished by covering it all with the leaves and twigs I'd brushed aside as I started. Then I arose and stood staring at the spot. I alone knew where this little fellow lay.

Suddenly a song from Sunday school flashed into my mind:

> God sees the little sparrow fall.
> It meets his tender view;
> If God so loves the little birds,
> I know he loves me, too.

Tears began to run down my face. I trudged home alone, composing myself. By the time I'd put my gun away in the shed and cleaned up for supper, I was ready to eat—until Mom put a plate of chicken on the table. I excused myself, saying I didn't feel much like eating.

Mom let me off the hook. "You likely got too much sun today. You're not used to it yet. Go on up to bed and I'll check on you later."

I got into my pajamas and lay down on my bed. Lying on my back, I pulled the covers all the way up over my head and grieved the innocent life I had taken. It was another step on the journey to losing my own innocence.

8

Stormy Night

By the time my twelfth birthday rolled around, the family had thinned out considerably. My mother, finally fed up with my father's philandering, had kicked him out, backed up by a court order to keep him away. Ken continued his career in the army, and my eldest sister, Yvonne, had become pregnant, married the father of her baby, and moved with him to a place of their own. This last family adjustment allowed me to move out of the hall into Yvonne's old bedroom. As an adolescent boy, I cared more and more about my privacy, and I enjoyed having a place where my mother and sisters couldn't intrude unexpectedly.

With our father out of the way, the tension in our home dropped considerably. We began to develop friendships. We had people over. Gwen's boyfriend, Roger, visited particularly often. At fifteen, he was three years older than me, and while I considered him a peer, I also saw he was at a different stage of life. He had gained a level of acceptance in the adult world that I had yet to attain. To my thinking, he was already a man, and I rather expected that one day he would marry my sister. When he came courting Gwen, I felt somewhat flattered that he noticed me.

He lived only a five-minute walk from our house, but sometimes— when he brought her home a bit later than usual and especially if the weather was bad—he'd spend the night with us, in my room. This suited his folks fine and kept my mother happy. Always strict with us about the opposite sex, Mom did her best to keep her children from getting into the kind of painful relationship she'd experienced with my father, and she made it plain that sex belonged in marriage only. Yvonne's having to get married shamed Mom deeply as she felt it reflected badly on her mothering skills. With Barb and Gwen sharing a room and Roger safely settled in my room, Mom could sleep in peace, knowing her baby daughter was safe from raging male hormones.

I still kept regular hours and usually went to bed around ten o'clock. Between then and eleven, the rest of the family would disperse to their sleeping quarters.

One Friday evening Mom was out working an evening shift, Barb and Gwen were on dates with their boyfriends, and Ronnie and I were home watching TV. After a couple of shows, I grew bored with Ronnie's choice of programs. He never tired of his favorites, whether they were reruns or new episodes. I didn't share his devotion, so I went to my room, turned out the light, got into bed, and fell asleep to the gentle sound of rain hitting the window. Sometime later I awoke, startled into full consciousness. All of my senses were in full-reception mode. Darkness cloaked the room. Stillness wrapped the old house. Yet something moved. Roger, in bed with me, had his hand between my legs and was gently caressing and fondling me. I flinched, and his hand stopped moving. Sensation flooded my body, beyond my experience and my imagination. Nothing had ever prepared me for anything like this.

Summoning all of my self-control, I relaxed and resumed the slow, deep breathing of a sleeper. I didn't know what else to do. Assured that I was asleep, Roger resumed his gentle massage. Unfamiliar feelings surged through my body and mind. Suddenly, powerful involuntary contractions seized me. Roger paused, then quietly removed his hand, rolled over, and lay still.

My eyes popped open and I stared, unseeing, into the darkness. I tried to make sense of what had just happened. I didn't recognize what

Roger had done to me for the abuse it was. I just knew that my friend, my sister's boyfriend, had invaded my personal space in an unthinkable way. His fondling had unsettled me, yet the release felt good. *Maybe all fellows did such things with their friends. After all, he is older than I am,* I thought. *He must know a lot more about life than I do.*

Roger drifted off to sleep, and the sound of his breathing, layered over the sound of the rain, eased my confused brain into slumber.

The next morning I awoke before he did, dressed, and went downstairs. When he came down later, we grunted a greeting but didn't talk. We didn't even look at each other. Somehow this most intimate of acts had put up a wall between us. I went through the next few days in a fog. I obsessed about what Roger had done to me. I lived it over and over. I felt no guilt, but I certainly felt uncomfortable. Something had awakened in me, something that needed to be attended to.

A few weeks later, I found myself drawn back to Roger. My mind explored the options: Maybe he would do it again. Maybe he would explain it to me. I needed to make sense of it. So one day after school, I went to his house instead of going home. I tried to talk to him about what had happened, but he didn't want to discuss it. What he did want to do was take me out to the garage. This time, he asked me to do the same things to him that he had done to me. Once again, those powerful sensations of pleasure washed over me. I left with a deep feeling of physical release and a growing bond with Roger, but I was more confused than ever.

Over the next few months, we sought each other out from time to time. Roger and Gwen eventually broke up for reasons of their own. Gwen knew nothing of my sexual experiences with Roger. After the breakup, Roger didn't visit our house, so I went to his place regardless of which one of us initiated an encounter.

Because of the lack of information and instruction about the traditional views on homosexual behavior, I still felt no guilt. I didn't think what we were doing was wrong in any moral sense. But I did feel a deepening sense of masculinity. I had a male friend with whom I had bonded and that filled the huge hole in my psyche left by my violent father and my absent brother.

Our experimentation evolved, and Roger introduced me to more activities to increase our pleasure, but we were never what anyone would call affectionate with each other. Neither of us was looking for love; our quest centered on physical pleasure. The bonding that resulted was a by-product. Yet as the months passed, I sensed a growing disinterest on his part. I didn't know why or even try to guess. I just knew he began turning me down more and more frequently, until I got the message that our sexual relationship had ended, and with it, our friendship.

However, that loss didn't turn off my need for masculine affirmation. Some of my adolescent male friends got that through sports, hunting, or fixing up old cars with friends. I wasn't gifted or interested in any of those things, but somehow that didn't bother me much. I'd found a way to get that deep connection with other guys through sex.

So as Roger wound down our relationship, I went exploring elsewhere. Here and there I found boys who would respond, though not with anything as lasting as my connection with Roger. These encounters tended to be isolated events, and I began to develop an ability to identify guys who would be willing and set up opportunities for an encounter. For example, when friends and I would go camping, I'd suggest to my chosen partner that we zip our sleeping bags together to keep warm. Some boys would spurn the idea; others were willing, and I would find momentary satisfaction in the dark. But those occasional sexual encounters always left relationships strained around the breakfast fire the next morning. The fellows I'd been with in the night averted their eyes from my gaze and avoided me in conversation.

Through my attempts to connect with other fellows, I began to get the sense that what I wanted might not be "normal" and that other people considered it "wrong." I still hadn't had any overt teaching at home, at church, or at school about homosexuality, but I became increasingly aware that regardless of how satisfying I found it, I needed to try to learn to live without it.

9

Upper Teen Developments

As a child I enjoyed attending our little Baptist church. Since my father seldom accompanied us, I could get out from under his shadow there. My mother, a solid Christian, did her best to raise her children in the church, so I got points from her for developing my spiritual interest. Pastor Donovan's gifts ran more to evangelism than to Bible teaching, but that suited me fine as a kid. His sermons touched me, and I became committed to following what I knew of the truth of the Bible, though with his emphasis almost entirely on the facts of the gospel, I didn't know much.

During my young adolescence I didn't experience tension between my relationship with Roger and my church life. On the rare occasions when Pastor Donovan would mention sex to us young people, it was always in the heterosexual context. He would warn us about "getting involved physically" without being too specific. Occasionally terms like "petting," "necking," or "going all the way" would be used, but we had to figure out those things for ourselves. Nobody gave any specific guidance regarding sex and sexuality. I felt content knowing I had never done any of those things with a girl, so I must be OK.

Eventually, though, my nagging doubts about my sexual interest in my male peers evolved into moral convictions—without, however, feeling the need to make a pivotal decision. That is to say, I gradually developed a general sense that same-sex sexual contact was wrong.

As I found it increasingly difficult to find fellows who were interested in intimate relationships, I also found it easier and easier to connect with girls as friends. Some of them were church friends, though most of them were classmates or childhood playmates.

I entered into the dating scene naturally. Like many guys at the time, I cultivated the Elvis Presley look. I grew sideburns and applied petroleum jelly to my thick dark hair so I could pull it back in a ducktail. I was blessed with an athletic build and dressed to show it off. From my earliest days of buying my own clothes, I liked to dress well and spent a lot of money on clothes. My efforts with my appearance paid off: girls enjoyed my company, and I liked being with them.

Some of my guy friends envied the attention I received. Early on, I discovered that girls like to dance, and I had a natural aptitude for dancing. I never went begging for dance partners. In an unexpected turn of events, my sister, Gwen, noticed my ability and asked me to teach her a few moves. From my perspective, dancing provided a level playing field for me to relate to her. As we jittered and jived, she wasn't older or smarter or better; we were equals.

Of course, dancing with your sister is only so much fun. I had lots of other partners. With some of these I developed a deeper interest. I enjoyed their company, getting to know them and what made them tick, as well as superficial physical contact like hand-holding and a good-night peck on the cheek. My guy friends had an inflated estimation of my sexual exploration with these girls. In fact, what happened in public had no correlation with what was happening in private.

While the other guys loved to share news about the scraps of feminine attention they were enjoying, I kept quiet. I knew the reason for this stemmed from a lack of anything to tell them; they thought it was because I made such headway with the girls that for me to speak of it would just make them feel bad. The thought of becoming sexually involved with a girl appealed to me but also unsettled me. I had several relationships that lasted for several months, and nothing sexual happened at all.

The only girl I ever touched in a sexual way lived in the neighborhood. Bonnie and I had lived within easy walking distance for as long as I could remember. She came from a large family, and on one occasion we were jointly babysitting her younger siblings while her parents were out. As we sat close together on the couch, something started to stir within me, and I put my arm around her. She snuggled up against me. I liked it, but it only made the feeling stronger. I recognized it because I'd had it before with Roger.

I moved my face close to her neck and became overwhelmed with her warmth and scent. I knew, from my friends' bragging, what came next. She hadn't resisted so far, so I tentatively slid my hand around to touch her breast through her blouse. Almost immediately I climaxed, and for the first time, I felt dirty. My mother would kill me if she knew I had touched a girl this way. Pastor Donovan would be horrified that one of his star young people would behave like this. I felt desperately uncomfortable. This was so wrong! Shame swept over me.

I pulled away from Bonnie and saw her look of bewilderment. I mumbled something about having to get home right away. She didn't get up to see me out. I still remember her sitting there on the couch wondering what had just happened. Once again a sexual experience had left me feeling confused. I couldn't make any sense of it. *Why did I feel so awful about something the other boys treated as normal?* What I'd been taught told me I had done something morally wrong, but somehow it felt even more wrong than that, if such a thing were possible.

That stood as the last time I touched a girl even remotely sexually until my wedding night. I liked girls as friends, but they unsettled me when they expected more than to be whirled around a dance floor, treated to a hot dog at a ball game, or escorted home after a youth meeting.

One girl in particular had serious expectations of me. Diane was the stuff of teenage male fantasies. At sixteen, she already knew how to make the most of her natural attributes. Skillfully applied makeup highlighted the smooth line of her jaw and her unusually large, blue eyes. Skin-tight clothing revealed a body that would have better suited a woman six years older. Sexuality radiated from her.

For reasons that defied my understanding, her attention fell on me. My guy friends envied me, teased me, and speculated about what happened when the door closed behind us when I walked her home from school. What usually happened, other than watching a bit of TV or occasionally doing some homework, involved her trying to get me to do what my friends suspected we were doing. The more assertive she became, the more uncomfortable I became. Usually I'd end up making up some excuse for having to leave and then beat a retreat.

The heart of our relationship was a dance partnership. From watching each other on the dance floor, we both knew we'd be a perfect team. I danced with lots of girls, but Diane and I fit so well together that other partnerships felt awkward. We began dancing competitively and enjoyed both the attention and the trophies we won.

My intense but short-lived relationship with Diane screeched to a halt one day when I walked her home after school. We both knew her parents weren't at home and I feared what she would ask for when we got to the door. Her fingers intertwined with mine as we walked up her driveway. When we arrived at the side door, she pulled a key on a chain around her neck from beneath her sweater. She unlocked the door and swung it wide to let me pass in front of her.

"Come on in, Bob," she said. "Don't leave me alone. My folks won't be home from work for an hour and I'll be lonely."

"Can't today, Diane. I have some things Mom wants me to do around the house."

"Aw, Bob, you can do that later. Just come in for a few minutes, please. I really want you to come in."

During this exchange she kept stepping forward and moving me along in front of her. As I tried to avoid physical contact, she kept getting into my personal space, which made me back up. Within seconds, she had maneuvered me through the door and out of sight of the street.

She put her left hand on my shoulder with her fingers resting on my neck. Her face drew close to mine so I could taste her breath. "Bob, I need you to come in today. Do your chores later. I want you to do something for me." As she spoke, her right hand fumbled with the zipper of my pants.

"Not today, Diane. Not ever!" I pushed past her and didn't turn around. I hurried down the driveway and onto the street. I heard the door slam behind me. That ended that, but my heart raced, preparing me for flight. As I rushed home, thoughts whirled in my head. *The guys would never believe I just did this! Why am I so frightened? What did she want me to do? Surely not touch each other the way Roger and I did! What would I do with her? I only know what to do with another boy! Why am I so disgusted? What kind of girl is she? I must never get into this kind of situation again!*

To help me keep that vow, I plunged more enthusiastically into my church life. I'd always been comfortable in the young people's group, and I joined them in some extrachurch activities such as Youth for Christ. I participated in every rally I could get to, joined teams, learned to preach, and gained a lot of satisfaction from that. Best of all, the girls in this social circle all kept their distance. I was known to be a fine young Christian man, and I did my best to keep my reputation untarnished.

I kept busy at school and began to work part time at the grocery store where Mom worked. It wasn't long before the store manager entrusted me with running the place when he had to go out of town for a day or two. I took great pleasure in teasing Mom about the fact that now I was the boss—that she worked for me. I'd tell her, "Now, Mrs. Fife, you'd better do a good job there or I'll have to fire you. Other women are lined up for your job."

She'd laugh. "They're not lined up for my job, Bob. They're lined up to pay for their groceries."

In the days following my eighteenth birthday, I felt more and more like an adult. Mom and I were closer than we'd ever been. I had graduated from high school, gotten my first car, and found a line of work I wanted to pursue as a career. Everything looked bright, and never more so than one day when Mom called me over to her checkout at the store. A couple stood there with bags in hand, ready to leave.

"Mr. and Mrs. Barker, I'd like you to meet my son, Bob."

She turned to me. "These are the Barkers. They run a Bible study in their home and I think you might be interested."

"That's great," I said as we shook hands. Before they left the store I had their address and the time of their next home Bible study jotted neatly on a piece of cash-register tape in my pocket.

The next Thursday evening, I took a second glance in the mirror as I dressed to go to the Bible study. I had abandoned the Elvis sideburns and had started wearing horn-rimmed glasses. Some people thought I looked like Buddy Holly, but that was unintentional on my part. I still favored form-fitting clothes that would show off the fruit of my hours of working out in the gym. I hoped that I would come across as a serious young Christian to the people I would meet within thirty minutes.

I drove to Ted and Lily Barker's home where they welcomed me into a tastefully but simply decorated living room. Five young people about my age were already sitting around, each with a Bible on his or her lap. I scanned the room and took the last available chair opposite a girl who looked to be about sixteen years old. She didn't look like most of the other girls I knew. She wore no makeup and dressed in a more-than-modest, casual outfit. She struck me as a wholesome young woman—attractive in an unself-conscious way. Her longish, blond hair framed a narrow face with startling blue eyes. Add fit, athletic, well-proportioned, and ladylike. That was my first impression of her.

Ted smiled broadly at us. "Several of you haven't been with us before. As we begin, let's spend a few minutes getting to know each other. We'll start with Audrey."

10

The Straight Life

My encounter with Ted and Lily and their home Bible study reset the course of my life for the next ten years. I felt a strong kinship with the other young people, especially Audrey, the girl I'd noticed at the first meeting. Her older brother, Jimmy, brought her with him from their small, nearby hometown.

The things Ted drew out of the Bible fascinated me. I had listened to Pastor Donovan's sermons for a dozen years and never seen the relationships among major biblical themes before. I knew the gospel inside and out. I had learned to preach it myself. I could walk you through the sinfulness of man, the holiness of God, and the reconciliation between the two which only comes through the cross of the Lord Jesus Christ. But Ted's teaching went beyond that. He showed us links between the Old and New Testaments. He told us about how Christ could be seen in the Scriptures long before his birth, foreshadowed in the Law and the Prophets. I was hooked.

I began to talk with Pastor Donovan about what I had learned from Ted, but I couldn't transfer my excitement to him. I sensed he only feigned interest. Finally, after enduring one of my rants about the days of creation, the feasts of Jehovah, and the seven churches of John's Revelation, he gently suggested that if this was so important to me, I should go to Bible college.

At the next study with the Barkers, I told Ted what Pastor Donovan had said and speculated that perhaps I'd be better off in another church, though I didn't know which one. Ted smiled warmly. "I would never suggest you leave your church, but if you're thinking that's what the Lord wants you to do, I'm sure you'd be welcome to meet with us."

My jaw dropped. I'd been meeting in the Barker home regularly for six months and they'd never even mentioned where they went to church, never mind invited any of us to join them. But Ted was right about the reception I'd get. The brothers and sisters at the Gospel Hall welcomed me into their fellowship. The transition felt smooth and natural for me, though Mom struggled with my decision to leave the Baptist church where I had been raised. For her, it was my family's spiritual home, and she felt my departure deeply. Eventually she came around when she saw that, rather than diluting my spiritual life, the new influences in which I had immersed myself made me even more zealous for God.

As well as enjoying my new church home, I enthusiastically participated in the Barkers' home Bible study. I confess that my eagerness to learn more of Ted's deep theological insights was matched by my eagerness to learn more about Audrey. The more I saw of her, the more she stood out from all of the other girls I'd known. She evidenced a deep spirituality and a mature mind. She grasped the concepts and connections we learned with an ease that made me envious. My family had never stressed education, so study and learning had never been a priority for me. Audrey's family contrasted sharply with mine. They valued the intellect and its development as one of the keys to spiritual growth.

The better I got to know Audrey, the more comfortable I felt with her. I soon learned that the way she presented herself at the first Bible study we attended masked nothing. She was everything she seemed to be. Naturally pretty, she didn't go out of her way to draw attention to herself in any way. For her, physicality was a fact to be accepted. The things of the mind and the spirit were to be pursued and developed. The girls at my high school were the opposite. They lived for the attention their bodies attracted, whether on the dance floor or on the couch at home after school; I can't recall ever having a conversation with them about anything of significance. But Audrey lived in a realm the other girls ignored, and I found this both freeing and refreshing.

With Audrey, I felt no pressure to even think about sex, let alone having to figure out how to avoid fulfilling someone's expectations. We threw ourselves into group Bible study and church activities. As we did, we inevitably got to know each other better and came to enjoy our times together more and more. We'd drive along the river and walk in the woods. We spent a lot of time at her home with her parents. Her dad, a First World War veteran, struggled with age-related limitations, so I'd sit in their living room playing checkers with him or find ways to help around the house. Both of Audrey's parents appreciated my attention and efforts.

Inevitably, changes came along during this stage of life. Based on my grocery-store experience, I got a job with the Food Market Corporation, and after a training stint in Toronto I was moved to Kingston. Until Audrey graduated from high school, our growing love conquered the geographical challenges, and we got together in the Trenton area most weekends. Life rolled along undisturbed in this way, and Audrey and I grew ever fonder of each other. Because we were both committed to keeping the biblical standard of reserving sex for marriage, we never tempted or teased each other sexually. We found the union of our hearts and minds to be a strong enough bond to keep us together.

Good student that she was, Audrey was blessed with several options at the end of high school. Fortunately, an opportunity to study nursing at Kingston General Hospital was among them. It didn't take her long to decide on that program, and within a few months we were closer together than ever as we lived near each other in the beautiful old lime-stone city.

As I hoped, our relationship grew at an accelerated pace, and toward the end of her first year of training, we were engaged. Even then we were careful to keep sex out of it. Audrey told me she took a lot of teasing from the girls with whom she shared living accommodations.

Unlike other couples who couldn't seem to let go of each other at the end of an evening, we felt no need of lingering farewells. The joy of sharing lots of time together as we poured our energy into work, school, and church fulfilled us.

As the wedding day approached, my apprehensions about sex in our relationship grew. I feared Audrey's expectations and my ability to respond to her. Before we were married, we did talk a little about sex and were relieved to learn that neither of us had a sordid sexual past to share with the other. I considered it unnecessary to tell her about Roger and the other boys I'd been with as a teenager. That part of my life was in the distant past and seemed entirely irrelevant to the present. I had never identified myself as gay or straight; I was just me, a unique individual with my own set of life experiences. I didn't even think about the past; I was consumed with my love for Audrey and my fearful anticipation of initiation into sexual intimacy with the girl of my dreams.

Once we were married, sexual activity with my new wife unfolded naturally though not immediately. Instinct eventually took over, and we were able to satisfy each other, though neither of us ever spoke of having had a "wild honeymoon." We added sexual intimacy to our relationship with no more than the typical adjustments all young couples have to make as they launch their life together. On top of our demanding jobs, hers in nursing and mine in retail, we were deeply involved in church activities and loved to entertain. Our first months of life together went by in a happy blur. But something about Audrey began to trouble me.

Most of the time our relationship seemed comfortable, uncomplicated, and unstressed, but sometimes I felt like Audrey was challenging my masculinity. When that happened I felt inadequate, sometimes even repulsed. The problem? I couldn't accept her taking the initiative in sexual intimacy. Sometimes, when I had been working late, she would have been anticipating my arrival home. She'd be ready with soft music, candles burning in the bedroom, and a passionate kiss as I came through the door.

Yet ripping off our clothes and leaping into bed with an amorous wife didn't appeal to me. I wondered what had become of my chaste, unassertive friend, and what was wrong with me as a man that she had to do all of this to be satisfied.

For a while this hindered our relationship. On one hand, I knew I should have been flattered that during the day my wife had been thinking about having sex with me. On the other hand, I somehow felt like less of a man when I arrived home to a wife ready to make love. Her expectations weighed on me. I experienced such insecurity in my masculinity that I couldn't deal with it, nor could I talk about it with Audrey. Nonverbally I sent clear messages that I wasn't interested in encouraging her aggressiveness. Gradually she accepted sex on my terms. Once we'd settled this, I again felt comfortable in our relationship.

11

Family Crisis

I cleared the on-ramp onto the 401 and pushed down hard on the accelerator. Moments before, Mom had called me at work. Her voice shook as she told me Ronnie had hit her with a stick and then rushed out of the apartment. She didn't know where he was, when he would return, or what mood he'd be in when he did, and she was afraid. I assured her I would be there as quickly as possible.

I tried to make sense of what she had told me in the context of our life as a family. Sure, Ronnie had exhibited the potential for violence when he had been teased by my sisters, but he'd never raised his hand against Mom. They had a particularly close relationship. She doted on him, making ample allowance for his disability, and he generally modeled sweetness and calm whenever she was present. He would do anything for her and was openly affectionate.

Ronnie could never have a regular job, but he took over my paper routes when I outgrew them and carried on with them for several years. Because of his strict adherence to routine, people used to say they could set their watches by Ronnie's unvarying route around the neighborhood. He always carried the heavy canvas bag full of newspapers over his left shoulder to make it easy for him to toss papers onto porches with his right hand. Over the years, this habit permanently twisted his back so that even when he tried to stand straight, his left shoulder always hunched up as if he were keeping a bag of papers from slipping down.

Because of his disability he never married, so he and Mom did everything together. After the rest of us were out of the nest, Mom moved to an apartment which she got for free in return for serving as the building's superintendent. She took this position so Ronnie would have a place to live and some meaningful work to do.

I struggled to imagine what had provoked his attack on Mom. She would never have teased him. I remembered how proud she was of him when they went to church together. From my place with the other young people near the back of the church, I would watch Ronnie and Mom down front. Sometimes Pastor Donovan had trouble remembering the number of a particular hymn. On such occasions Ronnie sat up, eagerly waiting to be called on for help. An unusual gift with numbers balanced his disability, and he knew the number for every hymn in the book. Finally the pastor would say, "Ronnie, can you help me out with this, please?"

"Forty-three," Ronnie would respond in a big voice.

Pastor Donovan would flip through the hymnbook to number forty-three and then look warmly at the face glowing in the front row. "Right again, Ronnie. I don't know what I'd do without you around here." My brother took great delight in the pastor's affirmation. He had few strengths to celebrate, and he'd found the perfect way for this one to be recognized and appreciated.

As children we all went to church with Mom, but as soon as the girls were old enough to flex a little psychological muscle, they found excuses to skip out. Ronnie and I sincerely enjoyed church activities and became fixtures at our little Baptist church in town.

I tried to imagine Ronnie and Mom sitting together in church now. I sincerely hoped Mom had exaggerated her account of what happened. *Had Ronnie really hit her with a stick? Others, maybe, but never Mom.*

Eight years my senior, Ronnie had a seesaw relationship with me. Because of his age and size, he clearly dominated me at first, but the social challenges of his disability led me to think of myself as his equal even while I was still a preadolescent. The confusion ended one day when I was fifteen. Ronnie had hit Gwen without the usual provocation, and I appointed myself to redress the harm. I had most of my adult size by then, and I physically pulled him out to the back porch. After telling him in no uncertain terms that he must never hit anyone again, I hit him. Hard. My right fist landed on his shoulder with enough force to spin him around. Shock registered on his face. The power balance between us shifted and remained stable from that day on. Ronnie knew I could back up anyone he might try to intimidate.

When I buzzed the apartment, Mom let me in and tearfully told me how she had asked Ronnie to clean up some garbage left in the stairwell before he watched his favorite afternoon TV program. Ronnie had become angry and, grabbing the only weapon at hand, a stick used for propping open a window, he lashed out at her and struck her arm hard enough to break the stick. The place on her arm where the blow had landed was swollen, hard, and discolored. Though Mom winced when I touched it, I could tell by the way she moved her wrist and hand that no bones were broken. Confident that she had suffered no serious damage, I assured her I would find Ronnie and bring him back.

I left the apartment building and began cruising up and down the streets looking for Ronnie. My frustration built as the minutes passed. Finally I spotted him. Head down, he was shuffling back toward the apartment. My usual sympathies for him were overwhelmed by my anger over what he had done to Mom. I rolled up to him, stopped the car, and got out. He had no idea I was looking for him and was so shocked to see me that he didn't even try to get away from me.

I flung open the passenger door and shouted, "You get into this car!" Perhaps remembering our earlier altercation, he cowed and slipped into the vehicle. I slammed the door behind him and returned to the driver's side, jumped in, and started off with a jerk. He could not possibly have missed my mood. After driving along for a block or so in silence, I turned to him and confronted him loudly. "What did you do?"

He wouldn't look at me and began to mumble haltingly. "She wouldn't stop . . . wouldn't listen to me . . . She made me do it . . . didn't stop until I hit her . . . I had to . . . She wouldn't stop." Glancing at him there in his misery, I began to soften. I knew Mom. The proverbial dog with a bone. Once she had something in her mind, she would just keep at it until you complied, if for no other reason than to get her off your case.

Nonetheless, I challenged him on his behavior and took him back to the apartment, and I stayed while Mom and Ronnie made peace. Ronnie apologized and promised he would never hit Mom again. Mom forgave him. I felt the matter to be truly behind them when I left a little later, and time proved me right.

That occasion raised my status in the family. Mom began to see me as an adult, and even my sisters accorded me some respect for stepping in and showing leadership.

12

The Wrestling Begins

My line of work, setting up new stores for one of the biggest food corporations in Ontario, necessitated frequent moves. Once the store was running smoothly in Kingston, I was sent back to Toronto for a year's assignment. Nurses were in demand, and Audrey was able to pick up work at Humber Memorial Hospital in Toronto.

Then in the latter half of 1969, the company shipped me to Owen Sound to start all over again. Audrey and I moved to this smaller town and almost immediately were confronted with another adjustment to make. Our love had produced tangible fruit: Audrey was pregnant. In happy anticipation, we made all of the necessary purchases and preparations.

We were happy together awaiting the baby's arrival in this small Ontario community. It suited us nicely. I liked the people I worked with, and once again we found a little church and developed a circle of friends with whom we could share our lives. We delighted in having people into our home, and we enjoyed visiting them in theirs.

We connected strongly with one particular couple who had a son just a few years younger than me. Jonathan became the younger brother I never had, and he looked to me as an older brother. I was twenty-seven at the time and he would have been about twenty. We were quite conscious of the age gap, and Jonathan sometimes teased me about being an "old man." On one occasion, we were alone in the recreation room in the basement of his parents' home when he started with his sarcastic comments about my level of fitness.

I had always taken pride in my strength, so I challenged him to arm wrestling. We gripped hands across a table from each other, and while I eventually beat him, I had to admit his strength surprised me. He could see I had only barely defeated him and pressed the point by telling me I couldn't take him in a fair fight. I told him that not only could I take him in arm wrestling, I'd put him down and sit on him to teach him a lesson.

In a flash, he jumped up, grabbed me, and pulled me to the floor, hoping the surprise would give him the advantage. For a while, as we struggled, it did. However, little by little I used my fifteen-pound advantage to wear him down, and it wasn't long until I had made good on my threat. I sat on his chest holding his wrists to the floor until he said uncle.

Though our wrestling started as a simple response on my part to his teasing me, somewhere in those few minutes as we wrestled on the carpet, I became aware it had become more than that for me. Memories from my youth flooded back—Roger, camping trips, strong young bodies, the intensity of raw energy unleashed. I jumped off him and extended my hand to pull him up, and as he regained his balance, I hugged him and clapped him hard on the back. "Well done, young man. Perhaps now you'll treat your elders with respect."

Even though I diffused the moment quickly, it unsettled me. I didn't want to feel like this with Jonathan. We were like brothers. It all seemed so out of place. Yet his innocence added to my excitement. Whenever I visited his home, I would taunt him about having beaten him and encourage him to accept an opportunity to even the score. Sometimes he did, and as we rolled around together on the rec room floor I would mentally relive my teenage sexual encounters, with Jonathan oblivious to what I was thinking and feeling.

Baby Sean arrived, and Audrey and I added the joys and challenges of parenthood to the seasons of our life. But almost as soon as our son was born, my work in Owen Sound wrapped up and we faced another move. We said good-bye to our friends and I paid my last visit to the home of Jonathan and his parents. I recognized that God had delivered me from a situation that might have become an embarrassment, and worse, to both of us.

Next stop: Rexdale, a community within the Greater Toronto Area. We packed up and made the move. At this time, I became assistant vice president of operations for the Food Market Corporation. That sounds quite grand, but in effect I served as joe-boy for Clarence Bullock, my boss. As well as overseeing the opening of new stores, I also executed operational audits of existing ones. At the time, some irregularities had been noticed in a couple of Toronto-area stores, and I had to spend time in them at night observing the night crew and checking over the numbers the day staff had submitted.

Audrey picked up a part-time job at a nursing home, which fit well with my evening and night work. We were able to share taking care of Sean, so that one of us was always with him. But working opposite shifts while caring for a toddler began taking its toll. Audrey and I still loved each other, but there wasn't much time or energy for intimacy of any kind, especially sexual intimacy. The quality of our relationship deteriorated into one that lacked mutual interests, hours of shared time, and passion for each other.

My hours alone with Sean and time on the road traveling to various stores gave me lots of time to think. I missed the sexual release I'd known in the first couple of years of our marriage. The logistics of trying to find time to be alone together when we both had even a vestige of energy made our attempts at intimacy feel mechanical and more like an obligation than a burst of spontaneous passion. Unbidden, memories of the past began to drift into my mind.

I began to wonder what was normal. I remembered the rush that came from my encounters with Roger. Was that normal? I wondered if all men had friends like him. What about girls like Diane? With the sexual confidence I'd gained through my relationship with Audrey, I thought maybe I had shut down something with Diane that could have been mightily satisfying. Did many people make it to their wedding bed as virgins? Was there really an external rule to follow, or could we do what we felt was best for us?

Maybe my upbringing had cheated me. I thought of the sexless years between the ages of eighteen and twenty-five. Was that normal? I'd look at people as I drove past them or worked with them and think: *When she was young, was she like Diane? Does that man have a Roger in his past, or maybe in his present? What would happen if I touched her? There's an attractive man; I wonder if he's as frustrated as I am.*

I thought it would be interesting to take a poll and find out what I could about people's sexual experiences, particularly in the areas of premarital sex and homosexuality.

13

Transition

Spring came early that year. The excitement of the passing of winter had inspired employees in a couple of stores north of the city to divert a little company cash into personal bank accounts. Clarence Bullock had assigned me to audit both stores at the same time. Because of their locations, he decided to put me up in a motel about halfway between them rather than waste his money and my time having me commute from home every day. I enjoyed this sleuthing aspect of my work, perhaps because it served to get me lots of affirmation from the men in the boardroom.

One night I was driving north on Keele Street after a frustrating late session at one of the stores, sure that at least one person on the evening shift had been tipped off and was obstructing my audit. I turned on the windshield wipers to clear the light rain, my mood matching the gloomy weather. I flipped on the radio and listened to Tony Orlando singing "Tie a Yellow Ribbon 'Round the Old Oak Tree" and gave in to self-pity. *Lucky for him,* I thought. *Too bad for me. I can't think of anybody who would tie a yellow ribbon 'round the old oak tree to welcome me anywhere.*

Ahead of me, at the side of the road, I saw a figure. As I approached, he stuck out his thumb. It was late; it was raining; I didn't think twice about stopping to pick him up.

"Thanks, man," he said as he slid into the passenger seat and closed the door. "Lousy weather out there."

"Yeah, it's no fun driving tonight. Gotta be worse walking."

"For sure, for sure." He squeezed the rain out of his hair with his hands.

A little younger than me, my passenger had a nice complexion and a warm smile, broad shoulders, and a straight posture without being stiff. He was clean-shaven, and his hair was cropped shorter than guys his age typically wore it. We introduced ourselves. His name was Lance.

"Where are you headed?" I asked.

"To my parents' restaurant at Keele Street and Highway 7."

"You're in luck. I'm staying at a motel on Keele near 7." I looked forward to having some company for the rest of my trip.

"Why are you at the motel? You a salesman or something?" he asked.

"I'm staying at the motel because of my work." I didn't want to tell him I was auditing Food Market stores in case the wrong people would find out. "Right now, I'm doing a survey on sex. Specifically, I'm asking people to tell me about their experiences with premarital sex and homosexuality."

I expected an awkward pause when I said that, but Lance didn't miss a beat. "Hey, man, you're in luck. I know some stuff about sex. Fire away."

I tried to make my questions sound clinical. "First we have to fill in the little boxes. You know, gender, age, marital status, level of education."

"Male, twenty-eight, single, fine arts BA from U of T." He rattled this off as if he responded to surveys every week.

"You said you know some stuff about sex, so I'm assuming it's stuff you learned firsthand. Tell me about your first sexual experience."

"Masturbated when I was twelve. Next question?"

"Tell me about your first experience with a girl."

"When I was sixteen, three of us guys decided we should learn about women. We didn't know any girls who'd be willing to teach us, so we threw some money together and hired a professional. We were going to each have a turn and drew straws for the order. I got the short one. By the time my turn came, I was disgusted. But one of my buddies looked pretty magnificent." He paused, looking for a response from me.

I tried to sound detached. "So no sexual experience with a woman at all?" I asked.

"Nope. Sorry to disappoint you. I just have nothing more to tell you in that department."

I waited for a moment and then asked, "What about the other department? Ever do anything sexual with a guy?" I forced my voice low to keep it from betraying my rising interest in what he was telling me. I found myself responding both emotionally and physically to his words. Something had reignited in me. I was pretty sure I knew how he'd answer. I was right. He told me he couldn't stop thinking about the guys he'd watched having sex with the prostitute. It got to the point where he'd fantasize about one of them in particular and masturbate.

After a while, he decided to take a chance with the object of his desire. Lance described how the boy had quickly responded that he "wasn't queer."

"But," the boy added, "I'll let you do oral sex on me, if that would make me happy. My girlfriend won't do it and I'm wondering what it would be like."

Lance shared the story with me in detail. By the time he finished, the "something that had reignited" had become a raging fire. He finished the tale by saying he'd found his calling in life—to satisfy men any way they wanted. It made him feel loved and valued. He laughed. "I guess you could call me 'a man's man.'"

Still trying to contain myself, I answered as coolly as I could. "Thanks for the story, Lance. I'll be sure it gets into my report."

We drove on for a moment in silence. Then Lance said, "Listen, Bob, I've got an idea. Are you interested in more stories like that for your report?"

"Sure," I replied, "but there's no time for another one. We're almost at your folks' restaurant."

"So here's my idea," he said. "Why don't I go to the motel with you? We can have a drink or two and I'll tell you some more stories and then you can drop me back at the restaurant. I'd be happy to do this to help you with your research, if you like."

"I am working against a deadline," I lied. "So if you're willing to give up some of your time to talk to me, I'll accept your offer."

They say a good storyteller makes his listeners part of the story. Lance was a good storyteller. I was a full and eager participant. We did everything I'd experienced with Roger and more.

Spent but exhilarated, we lay on our backs in the dark as dawn approached. Lance said he couldn't believe my last sexual experience with a man had happened more than ten years earlier. He said he felt sorry for me and regaled me with stories of bathhouses, gay bars, and the best places to go cruising for sex. I had no idea such a world existed. I could hardly believe that all of this was available and I didn't know about it.

After a couple hours of sleep in the morning, I took him to his parents' restaurant and continued on to work. I couldn't stop thinking about Lance and what he'd told me. I had to see the gay scene in downtown Toronto for myself. *Surely it can't be as wonderful as Lance described it*, I thought. That day, I became aware of all of the men around me in a whole new way and had to force myself to concentrate on my work.

At last I wrapped up my assignments, prepared my reports for submission, and headed home. As I neared our house, I began to think of Audrey and Sean. I felt ashamed that my mind had been so occupied with other things that I hadn't thought of them at all in the last few days. What would I tell Audrey? How could I justify what had happened in the motel? How could I explain, even to myself, what had happened to my perspective in the few days I'd been away?

But I didn't need to answer any of these questions. Several days of full responsibility for Sean had left Audrey needing a break. After a brief "changing of the guard," I found myself alone with my son. When he awoke from his nap, I fed him and we played together. By the time Audrey came home, life had returned to normal. She asked about what had happened while I was gone for three days.

"Nothing out of the ordinary," I lied. "Did catch a couple of employees who were fudging the books. Mr. Bullock will see to it they are dismissed. . . . Yes, I missed you too. . . . No, not tonight. I need to get caught up on my sleep."

I returned to my usual routine, caring for Sean, working at home and putting in odd hours as needed, and not seeing much of Audrey. One thing had changed: I longed to get downtown. I had to find out if Lance had told me the truth.

The opportunity came within a couple of weeks. I wrapped up a job earlier than Mr. Bullock expected, but I didn't report in. I called Audrey to say I had to work late and headed for Yonge Street with its sex shops, peep shows, and gay bars. I followed Lance's suggestions about where to go. To call my experience eye-opening would be a serious understatement.

I stepped from the May sunshine into the dim light of The Quest bar on Yonge Street. As my eyes became accustomed to their new environment, I got my first glimpse of the gay scene. In many ways, it resembled a lot of other bars, except for the absence of women. A line of men chatted and laughed at the long bar. Small groups of businessmen were drinking at tables. A few couples were paired off at smaller tables. And a couple of predatory-looking fellows were keeping an eye out for someone to hustle. After being on the road and eating in a lot of hotel dining rooms, I recognized this type, though they dressed differently than their heterosexual cousins did. I tried to not look like a fish out of water and figured the safest place would be at the bar. I ordered a vodka and orange juice from the matter-of-fact waiter and eased back on my stool.

The man on the next stool turned to greet me but repulsed me with his effeminate affectations. He asked me to tell him about myself, and I quickly told him I was just passing through and had stopped in because

I was thirsty. I gave no indication of interest in anything he might be prepared to offer. He looked disappointed and turned back to his previous conversation partner.

OK, I thought to myself. *We're not all the same.*

I lingered over my drink just long enough to observe some of the gay protocol that surrounded me. I could see there were signals to be given and cues to be picked up on, but they were meaningless to me. I'd have to learn about these things.

Next stop was The Roman, a bathhouse on Bay Street. A brisk young fellow in shorts and a tank top asked me how long I expected to stay. I told him I had four hours available. As I fumbled for the twelve dollars he asked for, he spotted me as a first-timer and pointed out the sauna, whirlpool, shower rooms, and lounge.

"Look," he said conspiratorially, "until you get the hang of this, just go have a shower, then find a cubicle. . . ." He provided specific instructions. "Remember, you're here to have fun, so don't get uptight. If I'm not around when you're ready to go, leave your towel on the end of the bed and put your key on the desk." And with that, he moved on.

Nervous and insecure, I watched men come and go for about three hours. I didn't see anyone I would call "my type." To be honest, I wasn't even sure what my type was. I found older men repulsive because they reminded me of my father. The young ones were, well, too young, boys really. I'd have felt I was taking advantage of them. I'd already discovered effeminate men held no appeal at all; they reminded me of ugly women. *Heck!* I thought to myself as one sashayed past, *I'm married to a pretty woman. Why would I want you?* At last, a tall, solidly built man paused by the door. He reminded me of Lance—a little younger than me, but with a seeming eagerness to please. I nodded. He nodded. I smiled. He came in and closed the door.

Before I knew it, my four hours were up. I tossed my towel on the end of the bed, put the key on the desk as requested, and returned to the street. One more stop today: Balfour Park. Before getting into my car and heading up Yonge Street to St. Clair, I stopped at a diner for supper and took my time eating to let the sun set. Lance had told me that things didn't start in Balfour until after dark, when the families had all gone home. A little after sundown, I drove to my destination, parked the car, loosened the second button on my shirt, and headed down a path to a wooded area. It was very dark; the glare of the street lights didn't penetrate here.

Out of the darkness a hand touched my arm. I steadied my nerves and looked at the man but could only see a faint form. "Looking for a little action?" he asked. Then, anticipating a positive response, he continued, "What'll it be? Your call first." I was taken aback. Somehow I hadn't expected such a direct approach. I wasn't about to engage in an act of intimacy with someone I didn't know and couldn't see. I mumbled something about having forgotten something in the car and headed back down the trail.

On the way home, I reflected on the day's significance. The last eight hours were full of firsts: I had lied outright to my wife. I had deceived my boss. I'd had a drink in a gay bar. I'd had sex with a gay school-teacher. And I had turned down an offer that made me uncomfortable. All things considered, I decided I'd made substantial progress, though I admitted there would be a price to be paid. I just wasn't sure when the account would come due.

14

Juggling

During the next several months I lived a lie. Everything about my life was a lie—to my wife, to my employers, to my church, to God, to myself. My whole life was devoted to me—me, me, me. I was selfish. Nothing mattered except fulfilling myself sexually, socially, emotionally. I would invent stories to cover my tracks, using extra work to explain why I couldn't be home in the evening and claiming home responsibilities to avoid work assignments that would tie up my weekends. I spent most of them in downtown Toronto, and if I missed one, I'd try to sneak some time on a weeknight to get what I increasingly saw as my rightful share.

Week after week went by with my duplicity exacting a high price. Some nights I didn't sleep at all as I tried to juggle all the broken pieces of my life—and at this point, everything was broken. I used every skill I had to keep all the balls in the air. They looked bright and shiny, glinting in the sunlight, but inside they were fragments. My relationship with Audrey was unraveling; we hadn't been intimate in months. I'd put my job in jeopardy by sacrificing my energy on the altar of pleasure. Long-term friendships disintegrated in favor of encounters in bathhouses that measured their duration in minutes. My relationship with God evaporated as I abandoned not only church fellowship but also all of my previously cherished personal spiritual exercises.

Yet somehow I kept juggling. I don't know if this was due to my becoming an expert liar or to Audrey's purity of heart and exhaustless patience. She trusted me completely. It never occurred to her to question all of the weekend work assigned to me. She never challenged me about the increasingly heavy load she had to take on with Sean's care as I spent myself downtown. Most other women would have given up on me, and I knew it. Some of the men I met in the gay scene had experienced this. Yet Audrey refused to complain. How could I shatter her illusions with the truth?

Then, after several months of shuttling back and forth between home and the gay scene in downtown Toronto, the first payment came due: I got gonorrhea. I dared not let Audrey touch me. She worked as a nurse in a senior residence. I couldn't let her risk becoming infected. I stopped at a drugstore on my way home to get my prescription filled. As I drove the rest of the way home, I sensed things were coming to a head. I can't say I felt guilty—at least, not in a way that would have affected my intention to pursue the thrills of same-sex relationships. I wasn't afraid of being caught, though I did feel uncomfortable as the tension grew between my family life and my gay life, between the philosophies that supported them, between the lifestyles, between the values. On a more practical level, I struggled with the fact that each demanded time and resources that robbed from the other.

Knowing that a crisis point was inevitable, I tried to calculate my losses if I gave up one life in favor of the other. With Audrey I was secure. I was a family man. My job was safe. I could relax. I would be able to reestablish my relationship with the people at church and maybe even with God. I would be what most people already thought I was. Besides, I loved her; I truly did.

But I also loved myself. I loved myself more. I was calculating what would give me the greater advantage.

I tallied up the benefits of my other life. In the gay scene, men constantly affirmed me as desirable—something I craved. I could indulge my love for the hunt. I had unlimited sexual interactions with people who were happy to please me with no strings attached. No commitments. No responsibilities. No baggage. Oh, except for things like gonorrhea.

I parked the car and went into the house. Audrey came to the door and kissed me warmly. During supper we made small talk about the day, the weather, Sean's latest exploits, anything as long as it wasn't important. After supper, Audrey suggested I put Sean to bed while she cleaned up the dishes. "After that," she said, "let's just go to bed and take some time for ourselves. Lately, it feels like you've sold your soul to Mr. Bullock. Let's forget our jobs and just enjoy each other."

"I'd sure like to just spend some time with you, but maybe before we go to bed we could sit in the living room and talk for a few minutes. I haven't been home much lately and I have a lot to tell you." She agreed, and we separated to our tasks.

I developed the growing awareness that the impending conversation was going to change my life one way or another. Empathy did not come naturally to me, but I couldn't avoid knowing that Audrey was likely to be crushed by what I was about to tell her. Though we had drifted apart, I knew I'd be upset if she announced to me that she couldn't be intimate with me because she had contracted a venereal disease of some kind from some casual sexual encounter. I shivered at the thought and shook it from my mind. That was all speculation. What lay before me was reality—life. My life. Our life. Everything was about to change.

As we sat down in the living room to chat, I glanced at the mantle clock and let it chime eight before beginning to speak.

"Audrey, there's something I need to talk with you about," I began.

"OK," she responded slowly, her intuition putting her on guard. "Is something wrong?"

"Well, not really wrong." I made quote marks in the air as I said "wrong," but after my mind spun briefly with the concepts of "relative wrong" and "absolute wrong," I thought better of it. "Yes, Audrey, I guess I'd have to say something is wrong."

I paused and waited for her to ask me what it was, but she didn't. "The fact is, I'm struggling with something. I've never mentioned it before, but I have to tell you." I paused and took a breath to steady myself. "Audrey, I think I might be homosexual. At least, it's only fair to tell you that I find men sexually attractive."

I watched closely to gauge her response. She maintained her calm and composure, and other than a look of deep surprise flickering across her face, she betrayed no emotion, certainly nothing hysterical or even dramatic. "Are you sure, Bob?" she asked.

"Oh, I'm sure." A forlorn little smile contorted my face.

"How do you know?" she asked. "I mean, how can you know something like that for sure?"

Although she already knew a few things about my childhood, I started at the beginning with the lack of healthy relationships in my family, especially with my father and brothers. I told her about Roger, about the camping trips, about my disinterest in being sexually intimate with my teenage girlfriends, about the fact that one of the reasons I was attracted to her was because she wasn't highly sexualized. Time stopped as the minutes ticked by on the mantle clock. I told her about Lance and my curiosity about the gay scene downtown. I spared her the details but wrapped it up by confessing I had gonorrhea, was infectious, and couldn't make love to her even if I wanted to, though I really didn't want to very much.

At some point, she started to cry. Then I started to cry. We wept together between attempts at having an intelligent conversation. It became clear to me that I still loved this gentle, loving, caring soul who trusted me and gave herself to me. She assured me that, since we were living in the 1970s, homosexuality could be cured. She was a nurse. She'd find a good psychiatrist and set up an appointment. She loved me. She didn't want to lose her husband. Sean needed his daddy. No one needed to know. We could work this out.

As she spoke, she was gracious, loving, and—maybe most importantly—confident. Confident of a solution. Confident I could be healed or cured or whatever it was I needed. Confident we could be a happy family again. The only thing that came close to being a condition on her part was that we would seek professional help together. Her sense of hope was contagious. As she talked, confidence grew in me.

As she talked I became convinced that I had to stay with her and Sean. I confessed I'd been unforgivably selfish. I promised her that when the infection had run its course I would make love with her again. I could do this. I felt a new strength. I didn't even think I needed a psychiatrist. Willpower would do it. I had made some bad choices, but everyone makes mistakes. I would choose to be straight. I would love my wife and honor my wedding vows.

By ten o'clock we were emotionally exhausted and went to bed. Lying there, within arm's reach of Audrey, I was amazed at the way things had unfolded. I had confessed my same-sex attractions to my wife and she still loved me. She hadn't kicked me out. She hadn't walked away. More than that, she wanted to help me. I was still a married man and the father of my precious son. Life would be good.

In the days that followed, I kept my word to Audrey. We resumed intimacies, though for my part it was rather mechanical. I spent my weekends with her and Sean, though I missed the excitement of the gay village. I started reconnecting with my friends at church, though they seemed rather boring compared to the men I'd left behind. Life returned to something resembling normalcy. With all of this, I disappointed Audrey in one significant way. Partly because I felt I could deal with things on my own but mostly because of pride, I refused to make an appointment with a psychiatrist. After all, I had broken my habit of visiting the gay scene. I had abandoned my contacts with the guys I had connected with there. I resumed intimacy with my wife. I enjoyed my time with Sean. I worked at building friendships. All external indicators signaled success.

But inside, a war raged. I could control my behavior, but my mind ran unchecked. Scenes from the past assembled themselves into private peep shows that I couldn't stop. Fantasies fueled by my same-sex desires plagued me. Regardless of how things looked on the outside, the inside was a mess. Even as I curbed my desire to act out, I gave myself permission to assess the physical attributes and potential availability of every man I passed.

The gay life called relentlessly. Yet at the same time, Audrey continued to be the apple of my eye. I didn't want to hurt her. I didn't want to leave her. I loved her.

But my life with Audrey was not enough. I wanted both.

15

Identifying as Gay

My harsh upbringing had some practical benefits. I learned to work hard. I learned to persevere. But I did not learn self-discipline. The good things I did were done because they pleased me at the moment or provided me with some direct if not immediate benefit. I guarded this secret well. Others looking at me saw me in a much more favorable light than could be justified. This, in turn, nourished my growing pride. *Look how people at church admire me. Look at my steady promotions at work. Look at Audrey's love for me. I must be a truly fine person.*

What do we expect to happen to great people? They get rewarded. I had spent the better part of a year devoting myself to family life. I remained faithful to Audrey. I cared for Sean. I worked hard. I made deep sacrifices. I deserved a reward or, if not a reward, a treat.

About noon, one Friday in July, I called Audrey and explained that a crisis had arisen in one of the stores in cottage country. "It looks bad," I lied. "Clarence suspects the manager is skimming from the profits now that the tourist season has started and more money is moving through the system. I hate to do this to you, especially on a beautiful summer weekend, but I have to go. I can't get out of this one."

Audrey believed my story. After all, I had been close to home for so long she had accepted what she saw as reality. Her husband had straightened up. He was affectionate, attentive, and sometimes even romantic. He had victory over his homosexual tendencies. And, amazingly enough, he had done it on his own. He hadn't needed a psychiatrist. He was a strong man. A good man. "See you Sunday evening then, Bob. Will you be home in time to go to the evening service?"

"No, Audrey. You know how crazy Sunday night traffic back to the city is in the summer. I'll be lucky to be home by ten or so."

That was that. At four o'clock that afternoon, I packed up my work, closed the drawers of my desk, wished the office staff a nice weekend, and headed to my car. I loved that car, a 1972 metallic blue Monte Carlo hardtop convertible with white leather interior. Chevrolet had only started the model in 1970, so there weren't a lot of them on the road yet. The car turned heads everywhere, especially when I went cruising around Queen's Park.

I adjusted my sunglasses, opened the top half of my shirt to the warm breeze, slid into the driver's seat, and turned the key. The big engine purred almost silently. I flipped on the radio and scanned the dial for some cruising music. I loved the music of the '70s. It always put me in the mood for an intimate encounter.

Approaching downtown, I turned the car south on University Avenue. The traffic crawled, since this was a summer Friday. My best strategy would be to park on a side street and see what came my way. I pulled onto St. Joseph Street, parked, and turned off the engine. I left the radio on; it helped draw attention my way. And I was looking for attention. My eyes darted between the windshield and the rearview mirror so I wouldn't miss anything.

A tall, slim man with a shock of blond hair caught my eye. He wore a neutral cotton shirt, mostly unbuttoned, and a pair of snug-fitting 501 Levis. I put my elbow on the window ledge and rested my hand flat on the warm roof of the car. As "Levi" approached, I waggled my fingers in the air briefly. He spotted me and approached the open window, leaned over so we could see each other, hesitated only a moment. "Hot afternoon. Want to go for a drink?"

"Sure. Hop in."

The thrill was back. I was cruising—in style. "Let's hit the St. Charles," I said.

"Great!" He smiled warmly. "I sometimes go there myself. Nice bunch of guys."

I parked the Monte Carlo in a twenty-four-hour lot with a security guard on duty and locked it up. We made small talk as we walked the short distance to the bar. When we stepped from the hot, bright street to the cool, dim interior things were just getting started. We surveyed the room and each other. He looked good to me. Masculine, confident, fair-haired, nice shoulders—my kind of guy. *Surely it can't be this easy*, I thought. We found an empty table and ordered some snack food and drinks. I ordered my customary orange juice and vodka; he ordered a beer. I always hated beer. To me, it stank. Time to look elsewhere.

Levi and I chatted for a while, and I kept an eye out for someone more appealing who wouldn't smell of beer when we went to some private place. He seemed happy to be with me and started telling me about his job in an advertising agency. He worked as a copywriter and sprinkled his monologue with clever lines he either came up with spontaneously or recalled from his work earlier that day.

Another couple of guys walked in. Like Levi and me, they were together but not together. I watched them go to the bar to order drinks. The bartender returned to them with a beer and a Tom Collins. I smiled across the table. "You said you come here sometimes, right?" I asked.

"Yeah, at least a couple of times a month."

"That's great." I gave him an exit line. "We'll probably bump into each other again sometime. We can pick up where we left off." I rose and headed to "Mr. Collins" at the bar. In my peripheral vision I saw someone else moving toward my seat. Levi wouldn't have to go home alone just because I'd moved on.

I learned that Mr. Collins had a name: Thomas. No joke. He was a banker, in the closet for professional reasons but looking for someone to spend some time with. We found a table in a secluded corner, and a waiter brought our drinks over. Thomas slipped a bill into the man's hand and we sat down.

After a bit of small talk, Thomas fumbled around with his suit jacket hanging over the back of his chair and produced a silver cigarette case. "You smoke?" he asked, revealing eight neatly rolled joints. *This guy is definitely into detail,* I thought. *Typical accountant.*

"No," I replied. "I've never done drugs."

He laughed. "You can hardly call marijuana a drug, man. It doesn't trip you out—just opens your mind."

I shrugged. I had to confess I was curious, but I hadn't taken the plunge.

He sensed my hesitation. "Hey, man, I'm not a dealer. I'm not trying to sell you something. I'm just offering you a treat."

He selected one, slipped the case back into his jacket pocket, and lit a match. The pinched end of the joint flared up momentarily as he lit it. He took a long drag, and then, holding his breath, handed the joint to me. Though I'd never done this myself, I'd seen it done lots of times and it all felt natural. After I took a long initial drag, I tried to hold my breath like Thomas had, but the pungent smoke irritated my throat and I coughed explosively.

He laughed again. "Take it easy, man. Don't kill yourself. Start a little more slowly."

I took his advice: just a small drag, hold, exhale. Drag, hold, exhale. My eyes started to water.

"You'll get used to it," he said. "You're lucky this is good stuff, straight off the plane from California. Some of the weed around here is mostly stems. That's a killer on the eyes."

Gradually I became aware that everything had decelerated. It seemed as if Thomas and I had been chatting for hours. The bar had filled up. The smell of food broke into my consciousness. "Let's grab something to eat. I'm starved."

"OK." Thomas beckoned a waiter.

As we finished our chicken wings, Thomas suggested we head for The Library, a popular bathhouse on Wellesley. I agreed and we left.

In the fresh summer air, my head cleared a bit and I felt a profound sense of well-being. I liked this. I would have to get some marijuana of my own sometime. Not now, though. Other thoughts were crowding my mind. As we walked to The Library, I thought about what a great guy Thomas was. He could be a real friend. It would be nice to spend the night with him.

In the bathhouse, we went to separate cubicles to get out of our street clothes, and I waited for Thomas to come to my door. He didn't. I went looking for him. He was in the lounge having another joint. I smiled. *When he's finished with that, he'll be good and mellow. A receptive, mellow fellow. How swellow.* I liked this feeling.

Back in my cubicle, I draped my towel across my lap and waited. The guys all looked better than usual. Finally one slowed as he walked by. I caught his eye and smiled. He smiled. I nodded, and he came to the door. "What do you like to do?" I asked. He told me. I nodded again. He came in and closed the door behind him.

And so passed the weekend. I forced myself to not smoke anything on Sunday. Memories of Saturday were a little fuzzy but clear enough that I didn't fear I had lost control of myself. I hated to lose control. Living with my father had taught me that having your wits about you could make the difference between avoiding or enduring something very unpleasant, so being in control was a thing with me at all times. And on this occasion I especially needed to be clearheaded when I returned home.

I showered, got into my street clothes, and left the bathhouse at about four in the afternoon. I found a restaurant and ate the first real food I'd had since Friday evening with Thomas. I wondered if I'd ever see him again.

When I opened the Monte Carlo's door, stale heat swept out. I had some time to kill and decided to go for a spin east along the waterfront, enjoying the fresh, cool lake air before swinging north to the 401 and heading west toward home.

Audrey and Sean were both asleep when I got home. Good.

Over breakfast the next morning, I talked about the miserable character I'd caught with his hand in the till. "He is a family man, well known in the community." I made it all up as I went along. "No danger of his making a run for it, so I didn't get the police involved. I'll let Clarence decide what to do with him. It will be good for the little weasel to spend a couple days wondering how his life unraveled."

I finished my coffee, brushed Audrey's cheek with my lips, waved bye-bye to Sean, and went to work. The office staff all looked well rested and tanned. Apparently we'd all had a wonderful weekend. Even Clarence's mood was positive. The vice president of operations had a smooth-running operation, so he left all of us to our usual routine.

During the week, I thought about the next Friday. As the days passed, my plan crystallized. I told myself what I had to do. *It will be difficult, but it has to be done*, I rationalized. *These things are never easy. You can't expect everyone to understand right away. Besides, this is best for everyone.*

On Friday I got home at the usual time, and as Audrey busied herself with supper, I went to our room and threw some clothes and toiletries into a sports bag. I slipped it under the edge of the bed and returned to the living room to play with Sean. At supper he fussed and cried with teething pain, so Audrey put him to bed as soon as we'd finished eating. While she was doing that, I retrieved my bag of clothes and took them out to the Monte Carlo. I patted the roof and said softly, "Come on, baby, let the good times roll." When Audrey came back from settling Sean, I was waiting for her in the living room.

She sat down with a sigh, but before she could speak, I started into my well-rehearsed monologue.

"Audrey," I began, "you know I've been trying hard to be what you want me to be. But I have to tell you, I'm not free. I'm not free of my homosexual desires. To put it bluntly, I'm gay. I have a strong desire to go back to the gay scene downtown. In fact, I've been back. I feel like I belong there. I feel more at home there than I do here with you and Sean."

Audrey looked at me incredulously. "But, Bob, you've been doing so well—"

I cut her off. "I would appreciate it if you would pack some things for you and Sean and go to your mother's place for a few weeks so I can try to work this through for myself."

"Are you sure, Bob? Is that really what you want?"

"Yeah," I said. "It's what I really want. I've thought about it for a while now, and I think this is what is best for you and Sean and for me. I'll call you in a few days to tell you if there's anything more you need to know, but right now I want you to pack some things and leave the house. When I come back in a week or so, I want you to be gone so I can think clearly without the pressure you're putting on me."

As I spoke, Audrey began to weep silently into her hands. Her shoulders were shaking as I turned and headed for the door. She tried to say something just before the door closed behind me, but I didn't catch it, and I didn't ask her to repeat it.

16

Making the Break

A week and a half later, I returned to our home on Elmhurst Avenue to pick up the rest of my clothes and anything else I thought I might want. As soon as I stepped through the door, I knew Audrey and Sean were gone. The silence felt supernatural, as if God himself had left. I was alone. I felt that. But I felt free too. My thoughts all turned to self-justification: I'd tried. I truly had. Things hadn't worked out for the marriage, but they were working out for me, and that had to count for something. Of course I didn't want to hurt Audrey, but remaining together would be as miserable for her as it would be for me. Divorced, she could get on with her life and I could live as I pleased without having to worry about anyone else. I had no one to take care of but myself.

I walked through the house looking at everything we'd acquired in five years of marriage, along with everything we'd brought with us when we'd joined our lives. I'd thought it would be difficult to decide what Audrey should get and what I would keep, but it wasn't. In that moment, in light of the life that lay before me, nothing behind me seemed to have any value. My books, many of them theological references? *You can keep what you want and give away the rest, Audrey.* The furniture? *I truly don't care what you do with any of it.* Kitchen appliances? *I don't need any of that stuff. Keep it or pitch it.* The bank account? *Clean it out and open an account of your own. You'll need a little money to get started with your new life.*

I'd give everything to Audrey. The only things I'd keep would be my clothes and the car. I kept the car only because I needed a way of getting away—away from this confusing, tumultuous double life. By the end of the month I'd called Audrey and settled things with her. I'd been in touch with the landlord and made arrangements to get out of the lease. I'd taken my clothes and moved in with a buddy. At thirty years of age I saw a brand-new life stretching out before me.

Len's apartment at Keele and Lawrence became the hub of my life. I could pick up guys anywhere with the assurance that I could bring them back there for drugs, sex, movies, food—whatever seemed good at the time. Len had a lot of experience with drugs and introduced me to strawberry acid, purple dot, and other soft drugs. We had a reliable source for marijuana, and I took full advantage of my newfound freedom. Only one thing spoiled it.

On two occasions, while I was at work, Audrey and Ted Barker drove all the way from Trenton to try to talk with me. Len was home both times, and he passed along their messages—that they cared about me, that they hoped I'd get in touch with them, that restoration was still possible. I was glad I missed their visits, and I never made contact as they requested. I didn't like being reminded of what I wanted to forget.

One evening Len and I were hanging out together, preparing to smoke a little pot and watch some TV, when the phone rang. I picked it up and bristled as I heard the voice of my sister Gwen. I had no idea any of my family knew where I was or what I was doing. I steeled myself for the worst. Recalling the feelings of rejection from my family in my childhood, I expected she'd rip into me. With all of these thoughts flooding through my mind, it took me a moment to focus on what she was saying.

". . . So when Audrey called and told us you've decided you're gay, I thought I'd better get in touch with you right away."

"Audrey told you I'm gay?" I asked.

"She's hoping we can 'talk some sense into you,' as she put it."

"Well, there's something you need to know, Gwen. I'm not interested in pursuing anything but my own choices at this point in time." I spoke emphatically. "I'm finding my way, and I don't want to be interrupted by family obligations or pressures."

She started to say something, but I cut her off. "No, no, no, Gwen. You need to listen to me here. If I have to make a choice here, I'm choosing where I'm at now over my family."

Gwen's voice came back sharply. "Now you listen to me, Bob. I'm calling to tell you, you don't need to make that choice. We're with you and we support you."

Speechless, I waited for her words to sink in. I never would have expected this from anyone in my family. Then, with the parameters established, Gwen and I had a nice little chat, bringing each other up to date on our lives. She told me about her family; I told her about my job. She told me about their house; I told her about the apartment. It was all very civil. No, it was more than civil. It was pleasant. I hung up the phone marveling that another hurdle had been crossed. And easily too.

Without Audrey to go home to, I kept whatever hours I chose. I could not get enough of the excitement that came from finding men who were willing to be intimate with me. On a given evening, I might go to as many as three different bars and a bathhouse, sometimes two bathhouses, before finishing off the night with a stroll through a park. Whether or not I actually had a sexual encounter was beside the point. I could go home knowing that, on that night, I had been with four or five men who were willing to be intimate with me. I thought of it in fisherman's terms of "catch and release." Once I had reeled somebody in, I'd let him down gently and then be off to see who else I could seduce. Then I'd repeat the cycle.

Often I'd find myself the object of someone's interest. In the gay community we weren't too subtle about communicating directly with looks, body language, and even verbal come-ons. I didn't find this appealing. I wasn't interested in being the prey; I saw myself as the predator. If the hunting was too easy in one place, I'd go elsewhere to find a greater challenge. I also wasn't into bondage, sadomasochism, or role-playing. If a potential partner signaled his desire for something that didn't interest me, I moved on immediately.

I had a psychological need to be in control. That's probably why I went easy on the drugs. I was a regular user, to be sure, but I didn't like to put myself in a vulnerable position and hardly ever would let myself get into a state where I couldn't remember who I'd been with or what I'd done the night before.

The development of my identity as a gay man paralleled the flowering of the gay scene in Toronto in the 1970s. It was an exciting time with real risk of police crackdowns. On one occasion I'd been at The Club until two in the morning. The next day I found out the police had raided it at three. Did that make me hesitate to go to a bathhouse that night? Not at all!

But it wasn't just the police who made life difficult for us. Gay bashing still occurred, particularly in the parks. One day a friend and I were identified by half a dozen men looking for some gays to beat up. When we spotted the impending attack, we jumped on our bicycles and rode for our skins. Fortunately for us, they were on foot and we evaded them. Did that keep me out of the parks? No!

The danger just increased the appeal. We all knew we were taking risks; they added to the excitement. Men came from far and near to be part of the action for a night or a weekend, so fresh faces showed up regularly in the bars and bathhouses. This suited me well because, while I wasn't into anything I considered kinky, I did like surprises within limits. If a new guy got too specific about what he wanted, I'd ditch him and find somebody else to take home with me that night.

The weeks rolled by and I loved my life of pleasure. Between the stimulants I took to keep myself going and the almost constant adrenaline rush that came with being in a state of perpetual sexual arousal, I had to get by on little sleep. It wasn't uncommon for me to catch only a couple of hours at home in bed before the alarm would signal the time for me to head off to work.

I enjoyed my work. Fresh challenges faced me regularly. As soon as I'd get one store operating smoothly, raking in a nice profit margin, I'd be off to work on another one. The problems that confronted me at every turn forced me to think fast and work efficiently. I also had to overcome resistance from managers and staff sometimes as I introduced sweeping change to their comfortable little world. This gave me opportunities to hone my management skills. The work required enough from me that I never got bored.

Because I valued my job for both its psychological and financial payoffs, I kept my sexual appetite under control while at work. Of course I did some serious looking. I made a mental list of the guys who were my type. But I always kept things professional. Nothing in the way I talked or acted would mark me as gay. I knew old Clarence and the suits around the board table would never tolerate it. The gay community was fighting to change that, but they hadn't won those the battles yet.

One memorable job involved completely revamping a store in the Yonge and Steeles area while it was still open for business. The logistics of that kind of project were complex, so I set up an office on the mezzanine level, from which I had a bird's-eye view of everything. On one particular afternoon, as I worked at my desk, one of the cashiers knocked and announced that someone at customer service wanted to talk to me. I stood up to see who it was and froze. My sister Gwen and her husband, Tony, were flipping through magazines as they waited. Wondering what on earth could have motivated them to drive to Toronto to see me, I went down to meet them.

Each of them gave me a big hug, and Gwen said they wanted to take me out for supper. So I quickly wrapped up my day's work and rejoined them. We walked to a nearby restaurant, where we talked about my ending my marriage with Audrey and my decision to embrace the gay scene. Once we'd discussed it all thoroughly, they assured me that blood runs a lot thicker than water, that I was still part of the family, and that they were not going to disown me. They offered to be of any help they could but said they didn't want to spook me and make me run away.

This overture of family solidarity caught me completely off guard. I'd never experienced anything like it before in my life. It seemed weird to me that after all those years of trying to have relationships and feeling rejected, now, after I'd done something that often split families, they were embracing me. They told me they were not against Audrey and wanted to support her and Sean too, but if they had to make a choice between Audrey and me, they would side with me.

This gave me confidence to reconnect with my family in a way I hadn't for several years. I'm not sure my dear mother, bless her heart, even knew what "homosexual" meant. I went to visit her one weekend, and we made the usual chitchat and got caught up with each other's lives. At what seemed an appropriate moment, I mentioned I had decided I was a homosexual. I didn't think I wanted to get into what "gay" meant. She didn't flicker. Either she didn't get it or she couldn't bring herself to deal with it. At any rate, once we'd put that out of the way, we didn't have anything much to talk about, and after about four hours I grew bored and lamented to myself that there wasn't a gay bar in town to which I could escape for a few hours.

For want of a better way to put it, I was obsessed with sex. I couldn't even spend a day with my mother without wishing I was out cruising instead.

17

Spreading My Wings

That spring my work took me to a store in Cooksville, a village that had been swallowed up by the growing city of Mississauga. Everything was progressing according to plan, and Clarence had scheduled a visit on that Monday morning to look things over for himself. He did what he needed to do and then came to my office to fill me in on the next aspect of the job. As I sat at my desk going over orders the manager had submitted to me, Clarence strode in and took his customary place in front of my desk.

I looked up at him and smiled. He got straight to the point. "Bob, you were seen coming out of a gay bar on Yonge Street on Saturday night. What have you got to say for yourself?"

Clarence was always direct, but this time it was more than just irritating. It was offensive, and I simply replied, "So?"

He seemed to consider that for a moment before announcing, "Well, you can't be a faggot and be my assistant."

"If that's the way it's got to be, then that's the way it's going to be." I locked eyes with him. "It's the same as with my family. If you can't accept me the way I am, then you'll have to do what you need to do and I'm prepared to live with that"—I paused briefly—"because I'm not changing to suit you."

"Never mind what I need to do. What you need to do is gather up any personal things you've got here and get out of my store." With that, he turned around and walked out.

So that's the way it's going to be, is it? Well, much and all as I like my work, bigger and better challenges await me outside of here, I thought. *I'm tired of being your joe-boy, Clarence. Good-bye and good riddance.* I gathered up my things, pulled on my coat, and walked out a free man.

I had saved some money, so I wasn't in a panic to get a job. I spent the next few weeks sitting in bars, visiting the tubs, hanging out with friends, and smoking pot. As the days passed, a plan came into sharp focus. I had flexed a little muscle with my family and my employer. Now it was time to spread my wings.

Provincetown, Massachusetts, is a gay haven with everything designed and decorated to appeal to us. Free to walk the sidewalks without fear, couples held hands, walked arm in arm, and were as affectionate as straight couples were anywhere else. None dared make us fear. Even the straight business owners knew that to turn a dollar there they had to cater to gay tastes, so they did. A lot of money changed hands in Provincetown. Many of us were professionals. Few of us were trying to support families. Prices were inflated because of the amount of cash floating around, but it was worth it to be in a place we could virtually call our own.

My experience as a food economist served me well when, after a few weeks, I needed to replenish my diminishing stash of cash. I found restaurants that were willing to pay me under the table, so I could keep all I earned. My knowledge of food and my management experience allowed me to realize my ambitions. And ambition filled me.

Lovely as Provincetown was, it was in New England, and New England has weather that can be downright unpleasant. So that fall I joined the pilgrimage to Key West. Other than the vegetation and alligators, things were much the same except for the addition of countless guys from all over North America to work my charm on.

My life became a blur, but I wasn't bored because my life had caught up with my dream. I had plenty of money, access to drugs, and all of the sexual encounters I could cram into my spare time, along with listening to music, hanging out with my pals, soaking up the sun, and working out to keep in shape. I could hardly imagine doing anything else with my life. Yet I wanted more.

As I moved about in the gay scene in Toronto, Provincetown, and Key West, I picked up bits of information about Europe. I bought a gay travel guidebook and started looking at maps. I needed to go someplace new—someplace where no one knew me, no one depended on me, no one would hold me back. So after returning briefly to Toronto, I bought a one-way ticket to London and escaped to Europe "to find myself," as I explained to the friends I was leaving behind.

From the airport I went straight to Old Compton Street, then the hub of Soho—the center of bohemian life in London, particularly gay life. That first evening I went home with David. We were both looking for something exotic. To a lifelong Londoner, a Canuck from Toronto filled the bill; to a fresh-faced Canadian wanting adventure in a world city, this gorgeous guy with the cute accent was a dream come true. We had a brief fling and then settled into a comfortable arrangement of my paying him a pittance for a place to live near the gay strip and his providing me with a pad I could return to between forays around the big city. I loved London with the gay version of its pub culture, but after three months or so I was ready for more.

Amsterdam blew my mind. Lots of the guys in London had been there for longer or shorter periods of time, so I had verbal descriptions of what to expect, but all of them faded before the reality of twenty-four-hour bars, live sex shows, orgy houses, and a vibrant sexuality that virtually spilled out onto the streets of the gay district. Everything in the big, gay sex establishments conspired to overwhelm.

Early on I discovered an all-night dance house. I walked through the front door attended by a sturdy young blond who took my money and my breath away. He pointed the way to another door that led into a long hall. Every step brought me closer to the pulsing beat of a kind of music I'd never experienced before. At the end of the hallway, a set of doors doing their best to be soundproof led to the dance floor. I opened them and stepped inside.

The room was full of men, naked to the waist, their torsos gleaming with sweat. The volume of the music was almost painful, making it difficult to distinguish anything but the driving beat that kept the men on the dance floor moving as if possessed. Theatrical lighting and strobes changed the visual stimulation at such a pace that I felt as if I'd already smoked a couple joints. Stunned, I felt the half had not been told to me.

Now part of the greatest dance party I'd ever seen, I pulled off my shirt and made my way to the polished hardwood. Spinning, stomping, and shimmying, I plunged into the dance. No one had a partner, or if he did, it was only for a few moments before another wide-eyed, glistening face whirled into view. We were free. We were celebrating. We were men. Together.

Eight hours later I discovered the back door, and, pulling my shirt about me in the fresh morning air, I tried to reorient myself and find my way back to my hotel. I had visited the bar, the tubs, and the orgy room, and I had discovered the pleasures of cheap Dutch marijuana. My mind slowly emerged from the fog as I walked to the room I would call home for the next ninety days.

During that time, I descended into total sensual abandon. Amsterdam offered absolutely everything my imagination could invent and more. Surprised to find ways to gratify my appetites that I hadn't even thought of, I plunged in. Amsterdam made every other place I'd visited seem conservative and uptight. But perfect as it seemed, I could only take so much of Amsterdam. After I had tried everything it had to offer its gay visitors, I was ready to move on.

West Berlin didn't lag far behind Amsterdam as far as I was concerned, though perhaps it was just a little more serious and businesslike. It somehow lacked the frenetic abandon of the gay capital of Holland. One of the things that intrigued me about these European cities was the extent to which English served as the lingua franca of everyday life, at least in the gay community. I was hearing lots of different accents, to be sure, but had no problem getting around with English and a smattering of greetings and survival phrases in European languages.

For reasons that escaped me, I liked West Berlin better than Amsterdam, to the point where I went looking for a job there. But I soon discovered that while English might be adequate on the street, German was the language of business. The Germans were impressed with my resume in the food and restaurant industries but made it clear that without knowing the language, I'd never make it.

Disappointed, I stayed for a few more weeks and then headed home.

18

Settling Down

I'd been away from Toronto for the better part of a year, and upon my return, in the constantly shifting gay scene, I found myself virtually an outsider. I needed to get a job, settle into an apartment, and resume the rhythm of life that had so attracted me in the first place.

Soon after my return, I heard about a sales job opening at Czechoslovak Airlines. I applied and got it. I found an apartment that suited me—one big enough for a roommate to help cover expenses—and began the process of working my way back into the community.

While most of my energy went into short-term relationships, say from thirty minutes to three days, I still needed friends for the sense of being connected to others in a meaningful way. My family all lived about a two-hour drive from Toronto, so I seldom visited them. The people I saw most often were my colleagues at work, but I always kept a clear line between the business and personal aspects of my life.

Somewhere in the back of my mind, I expected that one day I'd find Mr. Right and begin a long-term relationship. Since I spent a lot of my free time in bars and bathhouses, I mostly met men who were cruising for sex, not for a live-in partner. Private parties were different. At least some of the guys at those events were less into the bar scene and more interested in a domestic relationship.

Because my first roommate, Len, was well positioned socially, he connected me with a more upscale group of guys than I would have found on my own. They were known as the Rosedale Crowd, and among them circulated top athletes, politicians, university professors, and other community leaders. Many were still in the closet and couldn't afford to be identified in the gay village. They and their friends would get together to meet other guys and network in the broader gay community.

On one such occasion I noticed Steve. He looked to be about three years younger than I was. Blond hair, nice complexion, and a macho attitude. I found him attractive and made an approach, but it quickly became clear that Steve wasn't a one-night-stand kind of guy. He wanted a relationship. This, of course, presented me with a new kind of challenge which I accepted enthusiastically. I turned on the charm, and within a few weeks he had moved in with me. We were a romantic item.

I'd had roommates before, but this was different. Steve made it clear he wanted our sexual relationship to be exclusive, and I went along with him, though I chafed at his expectations. It reminded me of my marriage. He liked to know where I was and what I was doing. For him, these expressions of interest communicated affection, but while I felt complimented, I also felt controlled.

Inevitably, points of friction began to appear. I had learned to be exceedingly neat from my mother. She had high expectations of cleanliness and tidiness which I had absorbed, and I applied them to Steve. But he had been brought up differently. He wasn't a slob, but neither did his standards meet mine.

Sexually we were rather mismatched. I had pursued a promiscuous lifestyle. Thrills for me involved hunting down a desirable man who suited my taste in activities. Thrills for Steve involved having a loving partner who would try different things with him. I limited my promiscuous tendencies for his sake, but we began to fight over his expectations of me.

We hadn't been together long when we fell into a pattern in which periods of harmony were about equally balanced with periods of fighting. Yet somehow we stayed together. We liked each other as friends and chose to work out our differences. While committed to our friendship, I found I didn't like limiting myself sexually to him.

I discovered a technique that worked well for me. When a disagreement would start to escalate, I would goad him with my attitude and words. A feisty fellow, he always rose to the bait. I'd keep him going until he crossed the line, then I'd yell at him, "I'm out of here," and away I'd go to pick up somebody at a bar or the tubs. Steve, I knew, would stay in the apartment licking his wounds, trying to think of how to apologize to me if he felt he'd been in the wrong, or how to confront me if he thought I was to blame.

For all of the ups and downs of our relationship, we developed a close bond, and I felt Steve was one guy I'd like to take home to meet my family. Though a macho guy, he worked as the sales manager for a couple of lesbians who had established a solid little business in silk flowers. I hated the things with a passion and wouldn't so much as let them into the apartment. So I was not happy when, on the first occasion I took Steve to meet my mother, he took her a big bouquet of silk flowers. I expected she'd think of the gesture as "too gay," but she loved them, and with them Steve found the way to her heart. I introduced him to her simply as "my friend," and she went along with that, no questions asked.

By this time, Mom looked better than I ever remembered her. Something seems wrong when a forty-year-old looks seventy, but it was entirely appropriate for her to look like a seventy-year-old when she was seventy. Over the years, Mom had solidified a healthy self-identity which was evident in the way she presented herself. She perfected the art of applying makeup, got her hair done every week, and dressed as if she were going out even when she was staying home. Her posture reflected her new self-confidence and about the only evidence of advancing years was a limp that would manifest itself when she was tired.

Steve smiled at me and nodded approvingly at the vigorous little woman who led us to Ronnie's room, which he had agreed to vacate for us. For some time, I had wondered if Mom would let me sleep with a partner in the apartment. Now I knew. I felt proud of her but couldn't help wondering if she were as naive as she seemed, if she'd just chosen to turn a blind eye, or if she really had understood and accepted me and the choices I'd made.

Once Steve had Mom's approval, I introduced him to the rest of the family. They totally loved him—sometimes to the point where I felt envious. My sisters doted on him, and as he played along with them, my old feelings of rejection by my family came back to haunt me. During the time Steve and I were together, we made several trips to visit Mom and the girls. I chose to interpret their enthusiasm for Steve as their way of assuring me that I had their full, across-the-board acceptance.

Steve enjoyed his work and got along well with the owners, Marlene and Judy. He developed a friendship as well as a business relationship with them. On Labor Day weekend 1975 they invited us to join them at their little farm north of the city. The late-summer weather beckoned us, and it looked like a great opportunity for a romantic getaway with like-minded friends. I had purchased a brand-new TR6 earlier in the summer and loved to get out into the countryside with it. So after work on Friday, we threw a duffel bag in the back and, with the top down, headed out of town on the back roads to enjoy all the thrills the little car could offer.

With the roar of the engine, the blaring radio, and the wind in our ears, conversation was impossible, but we smiled back and forth a lot, bobbing our heads in time to the music and enjoying the journey. We arrived early in the evening and enjoyed the light supper Marlene and Judy had ready for us.

After a quick walk around the property we returned to the patio to enjoy watching the tall cornstalks waving in the warm breeze. Judy brought out bottles of gin and vermouth, a bucket of ice, a shaker tin, a bowl of olives, and four martini glasses on a big tray. We rose to the occasion and started into the evening's labors. By the time we each had a glass in hand, we were well into small talk about this secluded country place that granted all the privacy gays in rural Ontario could hope for.

We chatted about the weather, the cheap produce at roadside stands, and the height of the corn, downing martini after martini, our voices and laughter rising as the sun set.

Marlene commented about a woman who'd called to order a bouquet of silk flowers. "She wanted me to write some Bible verse on a card for her and send them over to Princess Margaret Hospital." She laughed, interrupting herself. "How cute is that? Fake flowers and fake encouragement coming all at once. I hope her friend cheered right up."

"Come on, Marlene, you know enough about psychology to know that both Bible verses and silk flowers can help," Judy countered. "Something doesn't have to be real to work."

"It's called 'the placebo effect,'" Steve chimed in. "It doesn't matter what you believe in. Just the fact that you believe in it does the job."

"I wouldn't say that," I said. "Believing in God does make a difference."

"I guess you'd know about that, eh, Bob?" Steve prodded me. Then he turned to the girls. "We should ask the boy preacher to tell us about God."

Instantly I regretted having told him that, at age seventeen, I had won a preaching competition sponsored by Youth for Christ. I had a bad feeling about the trajectory we were on.

"It's true," I said and retreated into silence.

Marlene jumped in. "I suppose it is possible a God of some kind exists, but he sure isn't the hateful, judging caricature you find in the Bible."

"That's right," Judy agreed. "Sometimes I think there is a God and he's kind and loving and generous." She paused. "I'd like to think I'll go to heaven when I die, and it'll be a lot like this, but without mosquitos."

They all laughed. I squirmed. I knew enough about what the Bible said to know they didn't have a clue about what they were discussing.

"It bugs me that Christians think straight love is better than ours," Marlene said. "All love is the same, right?" She didn't stop for a response. "In fact, I think our love is the most beautiful of all. Judy and

I understand each other perfectly. We're completely in tune with each other. Find me a straight couple that can say that."

"Look, guys," I said. "This conversation is making me uncomfortable. Let's talk about something else."

"Aw, knock it off, Bob," Steve said. "This is a perfectly good conversation. I want to hear what the girls think about love and God and heaven and hell." He paused. "I bet you know a lot about hell, Bob. I've seen your scary, big, black Bible. Do they make them black because they tell all about evil? Eh, Bob?"

"Shut up, Steve." My temper flared. "I came here with you for a good time this weekend, and I don't want to spoil it. God is a God of love, but he's also a God of truth and judgment. Tell the girls about the ride up here. Tell them about the horses we saw doing the jumps down at that equestrian center at the exit off the highway."

"Good idea, Bob. Those horses reminded me of the four horsemen of the Apocalypse. They'll come pounding down the road here any minute to usher in the end of the world, and we haven't even finished our drinks." As he spoke he assembled another martini. Then he threw his head back, face to the sky, and shouted, "Well, God, you're going to have to wait a bit. We've got some serious drinking to do yet this evening."

"Steve," I raised my voice. "Give it a rest or I'll go back to the city right now and you can either walk back or wait for the girls to bring you on Sunday."

Judy jumped in. "Some of those horses down there actually make it to international competitions. They are magnificent animals."

"We could go down there tomorrow or Sunday," said Marlene. "I know one of the stable hands and I'm sure he'd let us look around."

Relieved at this turn in the conversation, I relaxed a bit. We talked horses for a while—sharing stories (particularly of our first experiences with the big animals), jokes, and our limited city-slicker knowledge of horse breeding.

"In spite of the science and the statistics," Judy said, "horse breeding is like shooting dice. You can put the best stud and mare together and end up with a horse that just doesn't live up to your expectations."

"Exactly," said Steve, looking at me pointedly. "Sort of like a guy who says he's a Christian and has a big, black Bible, but doesn't live up to your expectations."

The girls began fussing with bottles and glasses.

"What are you trying to say?" I challenged him. "Why don't you just get it out here?"

"You're a hypocrite!"

"You're right. I'm a hypocrite. Now let it go, Steve."

"Aren't you ashamed of being a hypocrite? How can you keep that big, black Bible of yours and be my Mr. Wonderful? Are you still afraid of God, Bob? The 'fear of the Lord' getting to you?"

"So I have a Bible. You've never seen me read it. I don't read it. You want to know why I don't read it? Because it says I'm a hypocrite and I don't want to hear that."

With several martinis fueling him, Steve wouldn't let up. "So, Bob, you admit you're a hypocrite, but you don't have what it takes to stop being one."

"Steve, drop this. If you don't shut up, I'm going to walk straight out to my car, get in it, and drive away without you."

"But your God is a God of love, Bob. He wouldn't want you to do that. If you walk out on me, you're just proving you're a hypocrite."

"Listen, all three of you," I said. "Work with me here. We came for a nice weekend in the country. There's lots to talk about other than God and whether or not I'm a hypocrite. I'm sensitive about this. You're making light of something I think is pretty important, and I don't want to discuss it. I want this conversation to stop right now. And if it doesn't stop right now, I'm leaving. It's as simple as that."

"Aw, Bob, don't spoil the party," said Steve. "We all like you. You're a nice guy even if you are a hypocrite."

At that, I stood up, turned my back on them, and walked down toward the TR6. When Steve saw I was serious, he rose and followed me. Soon Marlene and Judy joined in the procession. Being the most sober of the four, I made the best time. I sat on the top of the door and swung my legs into the car, started the engine with a roar, and headed down the driveway. I could hear Steve yelling over the sound of the engine. "Come back, you hypocrite. Don't be a jerk. Come back and join the party."

When I paused at the end of the driveway to let a car go by, Steve caught up with me. He threw his head back, made a great horking sound, and spat in my face. I slammed the shift into neutral and jerked on the parking brake in one smooth move. I came over the door of the little convertible and squared off with him. Wiping the spit off my face with my right hand, I smeared it on his shirt. Then I curled my hand into a fist and drove it as hard as I could into his left shoulder.

The force of the blow spun him around and he fell to the ground. The girls arrived on the scene not knowing exactly what had happened but realizing that whatever it was, it wasn't good. Steve pulled himself to his feet, crying, and scrambled into the cornfield. As we listened to his receding steps, Marlene and Judy began to lecture me. I climbed back into the car, but Marlene stood in front of it, blocking my way and screaming that I had to help find Steve. I wasn't interested, but hitting him had dissipated my anger enough that I backed the car to the house and parked it.

We hurried to the spot where Steve had disappeared into the cornfield and, staying close enough together that we didn't get separated, walked through the rows of tall corn calling his name. Nothing. As the search wore on, the girls began fretting. "I hope he didn't cross the fence into the neighbor's field," said Judy. "Mr. Norris said he'd shoot anybody he caught stealing corn."

"Come on," I said. "Don't be melodramatic. Besides, Steve isn't stealing corn."

"She's serious," said Marlene. "We know Steve isn't stealing corn, but Mr. Norris doesn't. If he hears noises in his cornfield, he'll shoot toward them, and he doesn't care if it's a raccoon, the neighbor's dog, or a person. He's a bit crazy."

We tried to pick up the pace but were thwarted by the rough going, the fading light, and the effect of the martinis.

Just as we were deciding which one of us should go back to get flashlights, I spotted Steve sprawled on the ground. He stirred as I crouched down and spoke to him. He was drunk and exhausted, but we managed to get him to his feet. By now I felt bad about having hit him so hard, and I apologized to both him and the girls. We stumbled through the corn, cursing the sharp edges of the leaves and the biting insects that had come out in full force.

We didn't stop on the patio but went directly into the house, where we resumed our weekend getaway. Everyone made an effort to steer the conversation away from anything remotely spiritual, and the rest of the weekend passed without incident.

Even though we were good friends, Steve liked to egg me on and get me riled up. The tension that so often hung in the air around us prompted me to get away from him for a few weeks now and then. When I heard that a contingent of the Rosedale Crowd planned to spend a couple of weeks in Key West, I called Len to see if I could be included. To my delight, the group made room for me, and I began looking forward to the opportunity to get a holiday not only from work but, more than that, from my smothering relationship with Steve. He pouted when I told him about my trip just before I headed to the airport, but I had no regrets.

I loved Key West because it provided what I thought was the perfect social environment. We Rosedale Crowd vacationers were all cut from the same cloth. We all cared about the same things: having sex, getting high, looking good, getting our egos stroked, and living on adrenaline. Our lives were similar. Unencumbered by families and with more than an average amount of money in our pockets, we were free to pursue and be pursued as we wished without restraint. We all felt, *Hey! If I don't look after myself, nobody else will.* We understood the rules and every-body stuck to them. Well, most of us stuck to them.

We all chipped in and rented a guesthouse. Sharing kept costs down and gave us a chance to enjoy each other's company. By the third day, I had settled into having a great time playing the "it's all about Bob" game. I went to parties, stalked guys who appealed to me, got high, had sex, slept all day, and woke up just in time to get dressed up to go back and do it all over again the next night.

One night Len and I went to a dance club we particularly liked. When we arrived, the place was buzzing with musicians, writers, artists, and their hangers-on and wannabes. A handful of guys with guitars and conga drums carved a tropical rhythm out of the sultry air. Len and I shared a joint and then made our way onto the dance floor. The music pulsed. The mood sizzled. The cruising excelled. We danced at, rather than with, each other, preening and showing off. I tended not to focus on one guy for more than a few minutes. As I checked out the scene on the dance floor, I gradually became aware of Len's attempts to get my attention. I danced my way over to him and waited for him to speak.

"Steve's here." I could barely hear over the din around us.

I stopped moving and stared. The look on his face told me, "No joke." My heart sank. I'd come a thousand miles to get away from the guy, and he'd tracked me down.

"I just bumped into Pete, and he told me Steve has shown up at the guesthouse looking for you. Ian's trying to put the make on him, but he's not having any part of it," said Len. "He's asking everybody, 'Where's Bob?' You'd better decide what you want to do. He's definitely after you."

"Well, there's no way I want to let him find me," I said. "Too many people know where we are tonight, so we're going to leave here and get lost. I mean," I emphasized every word, "we . . . are . . . getting . . . lost . . . *baby!*"

We made our way out of the club, hailed a cab, and headed for the bars farther down the strip. The night passed in a blur of loud music, marijuana smoke, and beautiful guys hitting on each other. When Len and I got back to the guesthouse at about eight the next morning, Steve lay sprawled in an easy chair in the lounge. He roused when he heard the door and approached us, looking like he was trying out for the role of Knight of the Woeful Countenance.

"Bob, where were you? I looked for you all night," he whined.

"Come on, Steve, you're embarrassing me. Not here. Come up to my room and we can talk."

I most emphatically did not want to be alone with him, but even less did I want what was about to happen to take place in the lounge.

As soon as the door closed behind us, he started in. He told me he loved me, he missed me, he couldn't live without me, and he topped it off by declaring that if he couldn't have me, then life just wasn't worth living.

"Steve," I said, "I came down here for a few vacation days to get away from Toronto, the cold, work, and the old routine. I know you want to be everything I need, but I'm trying to get some perspective on our relationship, and your following me has made everything worse. This isn't working for me. I need some space. So just . . . just . . . cool it."

Steve was exhausted both physically and emotionally. He was vulnerable and pathetic. He begged. He pleaded. He wore me down. I relented. We picked up the pieces and hung out together until my "vacation" ended.

I learned some things about both Steve and myself from that event. His behavior proved he felt very possessive of me and wanted an exclusive relationship. I wasn't prepared to get involved in that kind of a setup, and I was more sure than ever that if the relationship were to survive at all, I'd have to engineer some breaks from him.

Late the next fall I heard Pete wanted someone to go to Acapulco with him. I contacted him and got the details. This wouldn't be a group—just the two of us. It sounded good to me; two would be harder to trace than a group. I told Pete I'd go with him, but he'd have to stop talking about the trip in public. He agreed, and we went ahead and confirmed the travel details.

Once again I could enjoy myself on the beach without my little shadow keeping an eye on me. I worked on my tan, watched for potential partners, hung out in bars, cruised, danced, and smoked up. Life seemed to smile on me. But once again, my vacation ground to a halt, cut short by Steve's showing up. Much more upset this time, I deliberately said harsh things designed to push him away—if not for keeps, at least for the next couple of weeks. I desperately wanted to get him back onto a plane, and I didn't care about its destination. But Steve, more determined to stay with me than I was to get rid of him, would not leave.

I hated feeling like I was trapped. I sure didn't want to hang around in Acapulco with him, so we rented a car and drove to Mexico City, where we spent the rest of my vacation time. Steve still worked for Marlene and Judy, and they had compassionately given him as much time off as he needed to "work on our relationship," so he had no deadline, while I had to get back to work at Czech Air.

I knew now that Steve and I were headed in two different directions. Ultimately we weren't looking for the same thing. He wanted what amounted to a marriage relationship. I was committed to the carefree, promiscuous gay life that had been the pattern for me from my first trip downtown.

Inevitably I broke Steve's heart for the last time and moved on to other less restrictive relationships. Steve found a guy in Chicago, and they settled down in Toronto in a long-term relationship that lasted until Steve died of AIDS.

19

Mom

Although the years I spent with Audrey were fading in my consciousness, I couldn't get beyond the reach of my birth family. I still felt anger over the lack of a relationship with my father and bitterness toward my mother for her emotional unavailability so much of the time. Memories of my siblings chiefly featured acts of petty cruelty that had wounded me deeply. I could stir up absolutely no love for them. Sometimes a random act or word on the part of one of my friends or partners would trigger an unwarranted response that surprised us both.

Some of my friends, who were better acquainted with me than most, encouraged me to get some psychotherapy. At the time, people in some social groups liberally dropped references to "seeing my shrink" into conversations; it was a status symbol. I still resisted the idea of seeing a psychiatrist, as I had when Audrey suggested it, though I knew I needed to come to grips with my past.

Occasionally someone would mention something called "primal therapy." They described an intensive, one-weekend session that helped them get on with their lives unencumbered by the past. The more I heard about it, the more attractive it sounded to me. It required a relatively small time investment and, according to accounts, got results. This therapy wasn't cheap, but it was certainly less expensive than biweekly appointments with a shrink over a course of months or, worse yet, years. I decided to sign up.

On the appointed Friday afternoon, I walked through the doors of a big old brick building in the Annex. Once all of the registrants were inside, the doors were locked. We were voluntary captives until Sunday evening when, full of insight and empty of baggage, we'd emerge to push forward with our dreams, unhindered by the dead weight of the past dragging along behind us.

During my first one-on-one session with a therapist, he encouraged me to "let it all hang out." He wanted me to go back as far as I could, dig up my earliest memories, and feel the sadness, pain, and rejection of my infancy and childhood all over again. Then he, the other counselors, and the others in group sessions would teach me to process my emotions, release them, and leave them behind me forever. My therapist suggested a few techniques for accessing my early memories, which, he said, "are often locked away because you don't want to have to deal with the pain associated with them."

After some more work with him, all of us came together in a group-therapy session where we used the memories of others to unlock our own recollections. Empathy and affirmation flowed as we recounted tales of our pasts. I realized that, most of all, I felt the absence of any recognizable expressions of maternal love. Since early childhood, I had wondered why my mother didn't love me. I tried to pinpoint what made me so unlovable and ached to find the answer. At this point in the therapeutic process, we were still owning our pain. In fact, we were hoarding it for a time coming on Sunday afternoon when we would go into a small, private, padded room to release the pent-up tension verbally by having conversations—albeit rather one-sided ones—with the people we needed to say things to. We would scream, cry, groan, or say whatever it took to externalize the shame and pain we had internalized as children. We would beat on pillows that represented the tormentors of our past.

I entered into the process wholeheartedly, and when my turn came for private time in the padded room, I had a few things ready to say to my family members. The single most significant "interaction" was with my mother.

"Mom, I've had an interesting time this weekend. I've learned a lot, and I finally understand some things that have been bothering me for a long time. I know now why I always felt you rejected me—because from the moment you conceived me, you *did* reject me.

"My father was a beast to you, and I've already talked to him about that and some other things. Neither you nor I were able to fight back or defend ourselves against him. I know he made you feel more like a thing than a person. He used you for his pleasure when he felt like it and abandoned you the rest of the time. That night when the sperm that would form me left his body and entered yours, you didn't want it. You hated it and would have flushed it away if you could have.

"Though you didn't know it, the next morning when you awoke and gave a sigh of relief because you were alone, you weren't. I was there. Someone to be treasured and nourished by your own body.

"When the morning heaves announced my presence, you had a focus for your contempt for the man who had used and abused and humiliated you for so many years. I understand that. But it hurts to think it was me.

"Remember how you used to tell me I didn't want to be born and how four doctors surrounded you and told you only one of us would survive? Remember the relief you felt to think it would all soon be over? Remember how, in what amounted to a medical miracle, they opened you up, got me unstuck, and pulled me, half dead, from your belly? It wasn't that I didn't want to be born. You didn't want to see me—this child who represented all my father was and did.

"And when they brought me to you, remember how you refused to give me your breast? Of course you had good reasons. You were too busy. You had other children to care for. You couldn't manage this extra chore when you had a job. Bottle-feeding was best. Of course it was. You could pass on the job to someone else—anyone who had a few spare minutes to stick a piece of cold rubber between my little gums to keep me alive until the next time.

"You don't need to be reminded about the rest. We both know you had no time for a little boy who wanted to be cuddled and read to. You were too tired, too busy, too preoccupied, too absent. I understand that. Your life consisted of almost constant emotional pain too. You were too sad, too hurt, too neglected, too beaten down. The last thing you need now is for me to reject you.

"So here's where we are, Mom. I've decided not to be angry with you or bitter about how you treated me. I've decided to just be sad, and not just for me. I'll be sad for both of us. Sad for what we both lost. Sad for what we never knew we didn't have. I love you, Mom. It's not a comfortable love, or a sentimental love, but it's love.

"Thanks for listening."

When the doors swung open that Sunday evening, I left behind the pain and sorrow I had carried from my childhood. I was a different person. I knew I'd made some bad choices. I knew that, in all honesty, I couldn't excuse them, but at least I could explain them to myself, if to no one else. How could I succeed as a husband or as a father when I'd never seen what those roles looked like up close? How could I be a normal, psychologically healthy man when my childhood had been anything but normal or conducive to psychological health?

In the days that followed, I continued to work through specific memories that came to mind. I knew that, as an intellectually competent person, I had to take responsibility for my decisions and actions, but rather than looking for someone or something to blame, whether myself or someone else, I sought explanations. If I could make sense of things, I could be free of the thoughts that crowded my mind.

The next time I visited Mom, she opened the door, and as I always did I dropped my bags and held out my arms to her. She responded with a big hug. I gave her a kiss on the cheek which she returned. I told her I loved her and she told me she loved me too. We went and sat down in the living room and had a good visit. To a casual observer watching our interactions, nothing had changed—the big hug, the kiss, the profession of love, the lively conversation. But I knew I felt differently about her. I still sensed the lack of an emotional bond but felt I understood why it wasn't there.

Over the next few weeks, as I reflected on this change, something began to gnaw at me. The primal therapy had taken me so far, but clearly there was more. I observed that with Mom, I always initiated anything emotional that might happen. I held out my arms to her and she responded. I kissed her and she responded. I told her I loved her and she responded. What would happen if I didn't make the first move? Would she offer me a hug? Would she kiss me? Would she tell me she loved me? I had to know.

Several weeks later I called her and told her to expect a visit. I arrived and rang the bell. When she opened the door, I just stepped in and put my bag down. After a moment she said, "Well, come on in, Bob," and led the way to the living room without anything more by way of greeting. We started with the usual "how are you?" small talk. That was fine, but the further we went with the conversation the more emotional I became. I hadn't seen my mother for several weeks, yet she couldn't even give me a hug or kiss of greeting. I felt my throat tightening up and had to blink to keep tears from overflowing.

Finally I spoke up. "Mom, there's something I've got to tell you."

"What's that, Bob?"

I paused to make sure she was with me. "I hate you."

It was an emotional slap across her face—and it got her full attention. "Why?"

"Mom, I hate you because you never show love to me. If there's any love that flows from you to me, it's only there because I express it to you first, and you just react to it. When I call you on the phone and finish the conversation by saying 'I love you,' you say, 'and I love you too.' But you never go first. You never say, 'I love you,' and allow me to respond. It's never you taking the initiative. It's never you giving me the love I need. The love I require. The love I want."

By the time I finished speaking, my words were punctuated with sobs. I spluttered away, my eyes and nose running, my face contorted. But we shared the pain. Together, we cried and we cried and we cried and we cried. We'd stop and look at each other and then cry some more.

When we were able to talk, we opened up to each other. She began, "But, Bob, you must have known I love you."

"No, Mom. You were a great provider. You gave me a roof over my head and food in my belly, but you didn't give me love."

"Bob, Bob, Bob, I worked so hard. You know your father didn't give us what we needed. I did that. I did it for you, Bob." Her voice, high and pinched, attempted to hold back another torrent of tears. She talked about staying with my father all those years when she wanted to be free. She rehearsed how hard she had worked, often holding down at least two jobs so she could keep the family together.

"I know that, Mom. I know now how hard you worked. I worked hard too. We worked together. No doubt you fulfilled your duty to us. But Mom—" Now my voice cracked again. "Mom, you never sat me on your lap, or patted my head, or put your arm around me and said, 'I love you,' or 'I'm proud of you,' or 'I'm glad you're my son,' or anything like that. I felt no affection. No tenderness."

I tried to reason with her. "Little children don't recognize a parent's hard work as love. They need touch. They need words. They need intimacy. That's what love looks like to a little child. It's what it looks like to me even now that I'm not a child anymore. I need now what I didn't have then. I need to feel your love, Mom, not just know about it."

There she was in her seventies, under attack and trying to defend herself. And there I was in my thirties, crying out for something I could recognize as affection from my mother. My words had shredded her soul. She had been so pleased with our relationship, with my going to church with her, and with my involvement in Youth for Christ when I was a kid. Later, I'd kept in touch with phone calls and visits. But now it seemed I had turned on her.

We kept hashing things out. Hours passed. We poured out our hearts to each other and connected on a deeper level than we ever had before. From that weekend on, our relationship grew and grew and grew. She learned to show her emotions with verbal and physical expressions of affection, and I responded with increasing admiration for this woman who not only gave me life but eventually was able to show me a thing or two about love.

20

Connecting with Sean

Maybe it was getting things sorted out with my mother that prompted me to think a lot more about Sean. Seven years had passed since Audrey and Sean ceased to be part of my life. After I'd sent them away, Audrey had set some boundaries regarding the kind of contact I could have with Sean. I'd heard they had moved out West, where her mother and brother were living. I tracked them down through mutual acquaintances and asked Audrey if I could see Sean again. She was firm. She didn't want some "Santa Claus daddy" blowing into his life and leaving her to fill the "mean stepmother" role. Yet this edict didn't stop me from thinking about him and wanting to see him.

I contacted Paul, an old friend from Toronto's gay scene whose employer had transferred him to Calgary, and made arrangements to spend a weekend with him. Then I tracked down Audrey and Sean's street address, and on a Friday afternoon I headed west.

On Saturday morning, I explained to Paul why I had come. He agreed to drive me to Audrey and Sean's address and, in effect, join me in a stakeout. I had no idea what to expect. I didn't even know if they were home that weekend, but I was determined to see my son. After more than an hour of sitting quietly in the car in a spot that allowed me to see both the front door and a slice of the back yard, I got my reward. Sean suddenly appeared at the back of the house to play.

I could hardly identify this eight-year-old boy with the baby I'd rocked, the toddler I'd soothed to sleep—my own sweet son. Unwelcome tears came and in the awkward silence, Paul told me I should go over and say hi.

"Audrey told me she didn't want me trying to contact Sean," I told him.

"Well, go to the front door and ask her to change her mind," he suggested.

"If I do that, there'll be no hope of building a relationship with him later." I continued to stare at the figure running about the yard.

"Does she have a court order against you?" he asked.

"No, but she has sole custody." I stopped speaking as Sean's gaze crossed mine for an instant. "I don't like being cut off from Sean, but Audrey said she'd let me visit him when he's older. I just have to be patient for now."

"Hey, man! It's your *family*. I think I'd give it a shot if I were you. After all, you've come from Toronto to see him. The least she could do is let you talk to your own kid for a few minutes."

I shrugged and kept watching Sean darting in and out of my field of vision. Now I was paying the price for decisions I'd made years ago. I didn't want to risk my dream of having a real visit with my boy by forcing myself back into his life unexpectedly without Audrey's consent.

I returned to Toronto with a strange mix of jubilation and grief. More aware than ever that I was missing Sean's growing-up years, I began expressing interest in spending some quality time with him.

When Sean was ten, Audrey agreed to let me visit him and made plans for a couple of her friends to join the three of us for a Thursday-to-Saturday visit in Calgary. I accepted her terms: I would stay alone at the YMCA, I would not try to be alone with Sean, and I would keep my Santa Claus impulses under control. In return, I'd get to spend almost two whole days with my boy. I'd get to know him as something more than a baby, and for the first time in his memory, he'd get to know me.

I stayed alone at the Y. I did not try to be alone with Sean, and, outside of buying him a baseball, bat, and glove, I controlled my desire to shower him with gifts. To make things as normal as possible, I got to accompany Sean to the optician's, where we picked up his new glasses. He looked handsome and mature for a ten-year-old.

The time passed in a whirlwind of parks, playgrounds, riverside walks, picnics, and cheap restaurants. On Saturday we went to Heritage Park, which offered a glimpse into the early days of Alberta's settlement. It devoted a significant amount of space to old trains, which Sean loved. So we played in the empty boxcars and wandered through restored locomotives, marveling at the machines that had opened up his part of the country to easterners like me. The complex boasted large playing fields, and Sean and I played ball together, taking turns at bat and pitching to one another. I thought my heart would burst.

At one point Sean announced he was hungry, so we headed downtown to find a place to eat. Audrey asked her friends, Dave and Donna, to take Sean into a restaurant and get him some food so she could talk with me alone for a few minutes. It seemed to me that maybe this moment had been planned, but I didn't mind. I was having a great time and didn't want to spoil it.

Audrey proposed we take a walk through the Stephen Avenue mall while Sean ate. I agreed. After a few silent paces, she slipped her hand into the crook of my arm. I felt downright uncomfortable. In the world I'd been in for the last eight years, such a gesture meant only one thing: somebody wanted to have sex with me. I didn't think Audrey wanted to go in that direction, but the gay mind-set had conditioned me to think that way. As well, Audrey's femininity made me uncomfortable. I wasn't used to being this close to a woman. We had lived together as husband and wife, but those days were long gone. I got a grip on myself and waited to see what would happen.

Audrey started the conversation. "I'm glad you came out here, Bob. It's a special time for both Sean and me."

I couldn't argue with that. It was a special time for me as well. Still, I sensed more on the way.

"Bob?" she said, wanting to be sure she had my full attention.

"Yes, Audrey."

"I've been thinking." She paused and I could sense her looking at me. "We've been apart for a long time."

I didn't respond. She was stating the obvious. I didn't think she needed confirmation of this painfully obvious fact.

"Bob, do you think we could get back together?" she blurted out. "You and Sean have been having a great time together. And I miss you, Bob."

I had not been expecting this.

"I've waited a long time to be sure I could handle this. I'd like to try again." She paused. "Of course, you'd have to want it too." Another pause. "You could start fresh here, away from all of the old temptations of Toronto. I'd help you. We could make this happen. Think how lovely it would be to be a family again."

"You know, Audrey," I said, more icily than I intended, "I didn't come here for this. I'm not trying to start over with you. I came to see Sean. That's what this trip is about. You're a great person. Truthfully, you're the best real friend I've ever had. But starting over? Giving up my new life? I just can't."

"But, Bob, that life isn't good for you. It's unhealthy. It's dangerous. It's not what God wants for you. I'm sure of it." She stopped for a breath and I said nothing. "Here you could start over again. Please, Bob, at least consider it. It's been so beautiful to see you and Sean together again. Imagine what it would be like to have this all the time."

I felt pressured. I didn't want to hear these words. I knew where she was coming from. It was a natural enough response, but I didn't want what she was suggesting. At the same time, I didn't want to hurt her. She'd already experienced abandonment once. How could she be proposing another attempt at something I knew couldn't last? In the midst of the delicate situation, I tried changing the subject and hoped she'd let it go. "Look at the time. Sean's going to be finished with his lunch. We need to go back."

We turned around and headed back the way we'd come. She removed her hand from my arm and we walked back in silence. As we neared the restaurant, Sean led Dave and Donna onto the street. Their eyes were glowing with questions, but they quickly read the situation and we headed to the car. At the Y, I said good-bye to Sean, told Dave and Donna how glad I was to have met them, shook hands awkwardly with Audrey, and told her I'd be in touch. Then I walked through the big oak doors without looking back.

The next morning I flew back to Toronto, picked up where I'd left off, and wondered when I might have another chance to see Sean.

21

AIDS Comes to Call

Teaching Sean to use a bat and ball in those few, brief hours we shared in Calgary was a thrill for me. I'd played ball myself since I was a kid, and I loved the game. From the early days of the Toronto Blue Jays, I was a big fan. Soon after I returned from my year in Europe, I got involved in the Cabbagetown Group Softball League, first as a player and later as a coach. My team played several times in the Gay Softball World Series, and we had some great times traveling to these events as well as hosting tournaments in Toronto.

In the spring of 1988, as I put together a gay men's softball team, an athletic fellow showed up to try out. Small but fast, he handled the ball well and was light on his feet. A former high school gymnast, he was a promising asset, so I put him on the team. I also took him under my wing, and it wasn't long until we were having a fling. He moved into the empty bedroom in my apartment.

Typical of my way of relating, he had barely settled in when I was ready to move on to other relationships. This hurt Wayne, but we had become good friends, and he decided to stay on, subletting the room. Ten years his senior, I looked out for him a bit. He saw me as some-one who knew his way around, and he used me to provide him with connections that moved him into some strata of the gay world that he might not have had a chance to experience otherwise.

One day after work, I got home first and began puttering around in the kitchen. As soon as Wayne came in, I sensed trouble. His breathing was shallow and he looked flushed. I asked him if he needed to see a doctor.

"I've already seen the doctor, Bob." His voice trembled.

"What's up?" I asked. "You didn't tell me you had an appointment today."

"It wasn't a very long one," he replied. "The nurse called me at work this afternoon and told me to drop in and pick up my test results. You'd be surprised how quickly they can tell you that you're HIV positive."

In a daze, I sat down heavily to collect myself. In 1991, HIV inevitably became full-blown AIDS, and AIDS was a death sentence. All of us in the gay community were losing friends to this syndrome which medical science seemed helpless to stop. Drugs were being introduced that slowed the disease down a bit, but the end result never varied.

I tried to comfort him, but he pulled away from me and shouted, "I've got AIDS, Bob, and you gave it to me."

I couldn't believe what I was hearing. "No, Wayne. It wasn't me."

"I've figured it all out." His voice cracked, high and tight. "I've been with you more than anybody else. I loved you, Bob, and look what you did to me. Now I'm going to die." The tension mounted steadily. "I'm going to die, Bob, because you're a tramp!"

Horrified, I tried to stay reasonable. "Wayne, it wasn't me. I've been tested. I'm not positive. It must have been somebody else. Think, Wayne. Who could it have been?"

But Wayne was in no mood to be reasonable and not ready to be convinced. We sat in the living room, drowning in a cocktail of negative emotions. Fear, anger, disgust, and sadness gave way to terror, rage, loathing, and depression. I began to fear for myself. Wayne was definitely HIV positive. I was pretty sure I hadn't given it to him, but maybe he'd given it to me. Each of us was worried about himself, yet neither of us wanted to be responsible for bringing doom on a friend.

Wayne's diagnosis brought the specter of AIDS closer to me than ever before. I had lost several friends already. Others were HIV positive and watching for the health changes that signaled the transition to AIDS. I was getting to know the staff at Casey House far better than I had any desire to. This groundbreaking hospice served the gay community exclusively, and we needed it. So many of the guys had been turned away by their family and friends, if not when they came out then certainly when they confessed to having AIDS. We in the gay community only had each other, and we weren't terribly useful when our friends needed the high level of care called for in the final stages of AIDS. I knew Wayne would end up in Casey House. His family had cut him off completely when he came out to them. We both knew what lay ahead for him.

By bedtime I had worked myself into an emotional state. I had lost friends to AIDS but hadn't seriously considered that it could touch me. My head pounded. What if I were positive? What would happen to me? If there had been a twenty-four-hour clinic within reach, I would have been there in a heartbeat. I didn't sleep much, and I beat the staff to the clinic the next morning when it opened at nine o'clock.

The two days until I got the results dragged by. Wayne and I were both under tremendous pressure. I feared for myself and hoped my test would come back negative. At the same time, I couldn't stop thinking of my friend. I genuinely liked the kid. He demonstrated talent on the ball diamond. We'd had a brief affair. We'd been roommates. I'd disappointed him, to be sure, but we'd stayed friends. I intensely hoped I hadn't infected him.

The test came back negative. I showed him the lab report, and that convinced Wayne I was not the one responsible for his condition. Even so, something had changed in our relationship. Before long, Wayne decided to move in with another friend.

22

Out of the Blue

In the late 1980s I worked at The Diamond Club, one of Toronto's biggest draws to its downtown core. People came from across the province to see performances by international stars like David Bowie and Sinead O'Connor as well as homegrown talent like Blue Rodeo. I took the job because of its prestige and excitement, but I soon found the work neither enjoyable nor satisfying. Everything about it was loud: the music, the promotion, the people.

To simplify my life, I decided get a different job working with my old roommate Len. He had a sign installation business, Sign In Please, with which he was struggling because of his battle with AIDS. I came alongside to help him turn the business around, applying my years of business experience in the food industry. I was living in a two-bedroom apartment on the sixteenth floor of a building on Sherbourne Street— an easy walk to Len's apartment and the heart of the gay village. To help with expenses, I invited a friend named Al to sublet one of the bedrooms from me. A long-haul bus driver, he wasn't around much; he just needed a place to serve as a home base.

In spite of the convenience of the apartment, I knew I had to make a big change if I was to make a success of Sign In Please. So I scouted a location on Broadview Avenue near Danforth and purchased it. The upside was that I could use the basement for storage, the main floor for retail, and the second floor for my living quarters. The downside was that it needed to be completely gutted and rebuilt before any of my plans could be put into effect. For weeks I spent every waking hour ripping out lath and plaster, old plumbing, and outdated wiring. The heavy physical labor was a shock to my system after my managerial position. I would return to the apartment, have a quick shower, grab something to eat, and collapse, exhausted, into my bed. The next morning I would drag myself back into a state resembling consciousness and do it all again.

One morning in the spring of 1991, a phone call jarred me out of my sleep. I slurred a greeting into the receiver, only to find it was a wrong number—some kid wanting to talk to his dad. The voice kept saying, "Dad, Dad, it's me," as I kept trying to convince him that he needed to check his number and try again. Suddenly, a surge of adrenaline brought me to full consciousness as I realized it was Sean.

I pulled myself into a sitting position. "Sorry, Sean, I was asleep. I just about hung up on you."

"I know. I thought you were going to."

"What's up?"

"I've finished my school year and after I finish up a few loose ends here, I'm going to do a little traveling. Mom's at the Summer Institute of Linguistics in Texas taking courses, so I thought I'd go down there for a few days and see her. And then, if it's OK with you, I'll drop in and spend a week or so with you on my way back to Alberta."

"Of course it's OK. When are you coming?"

"My best guess is that I'd be there about the middle of July. I'll give you the actual dates once I book my flights."

I fumbled with the calendar in my nightstand. "That should work," I told him. "I'm just tearing an old house apart, so my time is flexible. Get back to me when you have your plans finalized."

As soon as he hung up, I thought of other things I wanted to talk about. *Why do you want to see me? Is there a problem of some kind? What do you know about me? Does your mother know you're doing this? How are you paying for this?*

I looked wistfully at the receiver, replaced it on the cradle, and flopped back onto the bed. There would be no more sleep for me. My head was spinning with ideas, fears, plans, and excitement as I pulled on some fresh work clothes and started my day.

My work on the old house was mostly physical, which was a good thing because my mind could not let go of that early morning call and what it might mean in my life. Oddly enough, I hated to think of his doing any of the things I'd enjoyed so much. I'd be the first to tell you that the gay life was fun, but it wasn't a whole lot more than that, and I didn't want to expose Sean to it. After twenty years, it was feeling like a bit of a dead end. I often bragged that there were no surprises left for me. I'd done it all—at least, all that I wanted to.

Now here was this boy who needed a father and was reaching out to me. I began to think that to have the kind of relationship with Sean I wanted, I had to at least consider getting out of the gay scene. I didn't want to even introduce him to some of my gay friends because I knew what they'd be thinking, and I didn't want anyone thinking about my son that way.

Then there was the whole thing with God. I'd walked out on him even before I'd walked out on Audrey and Sean. I knew I'd need to get things straightened out with God because I understood, from my time with Audrey, that sharing your spiritual life is an important part of a deep relationship. I already knew I wanted a "normal" relationship with Sean. As a father and son, we'd share our thoughts, our desires, our plans. We'd have friends in common, activities we'd do together, projects we'd share.

As I thought about trying to be the kind of father I wanted to be to the son I'd abandoned years ago, I knew I'd have to make some changes. But how? I was immersed in a world that allowed me to be completely self-centered. I took what I wanted from people almost completely without regard for them. Of course, they were relating to me the same way, but that didn't make those relationships healthy, just less guilt-inducing. When I tired of a longer-term relationship, I cheated until I was caught. Then I moved on. What kind of way to live was that? There wasn't anything noble about it. I had a lot to think about.

Since my visit with him in Calgary ten years earlier, Sean and I had kept in touch by letter, and I'd tried to set up another visit a few times, but something always got in the way. Now, out of the blue, my son wanted to see me. In the six weeks after the call, Sean arranged a flight, I scheduled a break for myself, and Al arranged to be away on a long haul to British Columbia.

23

The Story Continues

Sean's arrival in mid July disrupted the more or less predictable flow of my life. He knew I was working on the house and was anxious to help. Working together was one way of making up for lost time. It allowed us to get to know each other. On top of that, with the strength and energy of youth, Sean was able to more than double my rate of progress on the project. Though he was content to spend our days working, I didn't want him to go back home without sampling at least a little of the city. So I borrowed a couple of bicycles and we spent a day exploring as much of Toronto as our stamina allowed.

As we zigzagged east through the city, we passed an unpretentious brown brick building in East York—Greenwood Gospel Chapel. I told Sean about conferences I'd attended there as a teenager and how we'd go out on the Danforth between sessions to hand out tracts.

"I think," I mused aloud, "when I have a chance, I'll drop in here for a visit and see if I recognize anybody from the old days." What I hoped was that someone would recognize *me* from the old days and help me build a bridge into the group.

Sean's visit with me hadn't finished sinking in psychologically when it was, suddenly, over. I parked the car and collected his bags from the back. Together we crossed from the parking garage into the terminal, becoming immersed in the confusion of people rushing to and fro with their baggage. Emotions ran high with the joy of reunion, the pain of separation, and the excitement of flying.

After he was checked in, we had a few minutes before he had to go to the gate. We chatted about the following summer, when Sean thought he could come for a longer visit, perhaps as much as a couple of months. Even while we were talking, my mind was busy. My week with Sean was one of the most significant in my life. Now my emotions were close to the surface as I realized that once again I would be separated from my son.

When the boarding call came, we were both startled. I risked a quick hug and managed to croak "Good-bye, son" past the lump in my throat. He stepped back, turned, and, with a wave over his shoulder, disappeared into the gate area. I stood staring after him, tears tracking down my cheeks. *I have a son*, I thought. *He loves me. I want to have a relationship with him. I'll do whatever I have to.*

My mind was conflicted as I drove home. Al was due back later in the day. He'd be excited about a weekend he and I had planned in Boston. The Blue Jays had a three-game series against the Red Sox, and we both wanted to be there. Juan Guzmán and Joe Carter were playing up a storm that year, and since we couldn't get decent home-game tickets, the next best thing was to get to an away game within short flying distance. Our hopes for the Jays were running high, and some people were predicting a World Series for the Jays within the next couple of years.

The trip to Boston still sounded good, but I dreaded what was planned for the rest of the time. After the games we'd get some food, cruise the gay bars, have a few drinks, and then Al would pick up somebody to bring back to his hotel room. I didn't have a clue how I'd respond when I was surrounded with opportunities to engage in the hunt in unexplored territory, so I was reluctant. Maybe I'd just go on autopilot and fall into my typical patterns. That was a possibility, maybe even a likelihood. Yet I'd just told my son that I wanted to get out. A lot of this trip did not fit into my new and still untested resolve.

In the end, I decided to risk going since the flights and hotel rooms were booked and, as I expected, Al pushed me to go. (I hadn't gathered my courage to tell him about my change of heart.) Neither of us had ever sat in the legendary Green Monster of Fenway Park; we both were looking forward to being in the historic stadium where so many baseball greats had played.

Friday's game was exciting, though the Jays lost. We left the park and stopped for supper. Then, inevitably, we headed to the gay village to go barhopping until Al got lucky.

The first bar we hit featured lasers, chrome, and mirrors. A sophisticated lighting system pulsed with the beat of the music. We approached the stand-up bar and ordered drinks. Within a few minutes Al caught the eye of a clean-cut fellow dressed in casual business attire. They soon retired to a booth to get acquainted, leaving me at the bar. Several guys signaled interest in me, but I never enjoyed being the object of the hunt, and on this occasion I resisted my usual impulse to try my hand at hunting.

After a half hour or so, Al returned to introduce his new friend, Jacko, to me. "Jacko, here, is a local, and he knows a great dance club within an easy walk. You want to join us?" The night was still young and I had nothing else to do, so I followed them out into the hot summer evening.

Inside the dimly lit club, a disco-ball scattered flecks of light over the glistening torsos of the men on an expansive dance floor. Two weeks earlier, such a scene would have provoked a very different reaction than it did that night. I would have had my shirt off and been among the dancers in a heartbeat. But something was different. I made my way to the lounge area and let the waiter bring me a drink while I watched the action.

Al and Jacko seemed to be hitting it off well. I was happy for Al because I knew I certainly wasn't good company for him. I didn't blame him a bit for ditching me. He was having fun now. I wasn't. I sat, feeling miserable, nursing my drink for a while longer, and then I signaled to Al my intention to go back to the hotel. He waved me off and I went out onto the street alone.

How could I explain my mood? What word would fit? Strange? Weird? Odd? Inexplicable? It had never happened before—ever. Plenty of attractive men drifted in and out of my line of sight, some even my type, but what would happen was all so predictable. Only so many variations were possible. I'd been there, doing that, for twenty years. Even the men all seemed the same. If there was a surprise left, it had to be this: my walking out of a bar by myself before closing time.

Saturday was a repeat of Friday. The Jays lost. We ate. Al went cruising. I returned to the hotel alone.

Sunday was better. The Jays won. But we didn't have much time to celebrate before having to head to the airport to catch the plane home. I was happy, but my happiness wasn't just due to the Blue Jays' victory. Mostly, I was happy because I had surprised myself by successfully following through on my decision for these last two days. I began to hope. *Maybe I can do it. Maybe I will be able to follow up on what I impetuously told Sean.*

24

What Have I Done?

The first night of Sean's visit had been nothing short of a miracle. Even though I didn't know how, or even if, I could make it happen, I clarified and solidified my desire to get out of the gay scene and be a normal dad to Sean. I believe God played an active role in the conversation and events of that evening, so that I gained the confidence to verbalize my intention to Sean in spite of my doubts.

I've known many people who have experienced a work of God in their lives, and none can give a purely logical explanation for what happened. All they know is, they committed themselves to God and something changed in them. They began to see and respond to things differently. Their values changed. Their attitudes changed. People who harbored murderous resentment toward someone else experienced a total change of heart. People who lived promiscuously became faithful spouses. People full of resentment and bitterness toward their parents found forgiveness and love. People who had written others off entirely found their hearts opened toward them. People who had sexualized every relationship began to see others as whole persons, not just as bodies to exploit for personal pleasure.

It didn't take long for my decision to begin to take effect. Till now, conflict in my life had been of the man-versus-man variety. It arose when others thwarted me from fulfilling my personal needs and desires, whether by trying to shape me into what they thought I should be or by getting in the way of what I wanted to be. Now the conflict shifted to man versus himself. I had committed myself to a way of being and doing that sharply opposed my own natural inclinations, which had played me false by not delivering the long-term satisfaction I thought they offered.

Now, instead of seeing nongays as the enemy, I saw them as allies in a new battle—one against myself. Right away I recognized I would need to recruit a group of new friends who would support me, not only by affirming my decision to change my life but also by sticking with me through the process.

I had been calling out to God almost constantly since the first night of Sean's visit. But though I had now aligned myself with him and knew theoretically about his forgiveness, I realized my faith was shaky and needed to be strengthened into full-blown confidence before I faced my anticipated struggles with the consequences of old decisions and patterns of behavior I needed to release. I needed new friends, and I knew instinctively that they would have to come largely from the ranks of people I'd ignored and avoided for the previous twenty years. I wasn't confident they would turn to me as enthusiastically as I intended to turn to them. Yet I had no choice but to take the risk.

When Sean and I had ridden past Greenwood Gospel Chapel on our bicycles, I had made a mental note of the meeting times. The following Sunday, I greeted the two men at the door and told them I'd like to sit at the back and observe. They indicated that would be fine and suggested I pick up a hymnbook on the way in. I hadn't held a *Hymns for the Little Flock* in my hands for a long time, but it fit somehow. I riffled through the pages and was surprised that I still remembered some of the hymns. The services that morning were much like those I used to attend thirty years earlier at the Trenton Gospel Hall. The people were friendly. Several introduced themselves and expressed some interest in me.

y back to my apartment, I felt comforted. Real hope con-
r. Though I couldn't erase the last twenty years or their
effect on me and the people I loved, maybe there was a way to make a
new start. That afternoon, I began to think new thoughts that gradually
replaced my sexual obsession. I considered what practical steps I'd need
to take in the next few weeks to effect the kind of total life change I was
convinced I wanted. I still wasn't sure such change was really possible,
but I was willing to try, and I surprised myself by acknowledging that
I'd need some help. That was a signal of change in itself. Until now I'd
been fiercely independent and would rather fail than admit I couldn't
achieve my goals on my own.

Several years earlier, I had given up smoking. I'd been a three-pack-
a-day man, and I often lit one cigarette with the glowing butt of the
previous one. My partner at the time, Steve, was increasingly concerned
about his health and decided to quit. He was so committed that he
enrolled in a program to help him. We both knew it would help him
if I quit at the same time. I didn't enroll in the program but walked
through it with him. In part, I did it for him, but I also did it for myself.
I had become aware that this thing I used to do for enjoyment had
become my master, and I hated the feeling of being controlled.

Now I faced a similar situation with marijuana. From my very first
joint with Thomas, I had become a committed user. Maybe I wasn't
addicted in the sense of feeling desperate if I couldn't lay hands on
a joint, but I certainly abused pot. I carried a toke box with me and
would use it many times a day to maintain a perpetual low-level high.
This allowed me to function normally in my workplace interactions
while maintaining the pleasant background feeling of hyperalertness
and enhanced perception that pot gave me.

Having decided to get serious with God, I knew I'd have to give
up marijuana. No one told me this was necessary; I intuited it in my
spirit. Without pressure from the outside, I became convinced that
there was no room in my life for both pot and God. With some regret,
I flushed my stash down the toilet. Part of me wanted to pretend that

an occasional joint wouldn't hurt me or anybody else, but I knew the stuff had to go.

I can't say I suffered from the loss of marijuana in my life. I didn't experience serious somatic symptoms of withdrawal, nor did I struggle much psychologically. Sometimes being in a certain place, like waiting in line to get into a Blue Jays game, or doing a specific activity such as listening to music, would trigger the thought, *I should have a joint*. But as quickly as the thought would emerge, I'd remember that I had given up marijuana, and that was enough for me.

While marijuana and other soft drugs had accompanied me constantly in my life as a gay man, I was able to set them aside without undue difficulty. But I knew that the core issue was something else. I wanted freedom from my particular homosexual lifestyle, but I didn't expect I could attain that freedom without help. I had seen contact information of organizations offering help to gay men posted in various places in the village, and I had read stories of men who not only had abandoned the external gay world with its values, attitudes, and behaviors but also had experienced profound inner change. I looked up phone numbers and began to make calls.

As I spoke with the men on the other end of the line and realized they had once been where I'd been but were there no longer, my hope strengthened. If others could make the journey, I could too. I selected a program run by a local ministry to gays as the one best suited to what I hoped to accomplish. Their meetings were held in a downtown church, and I soon enrolled in a program that featured both support-group sessions and one-on-one counseling.

I was assigned to Peter, a godly young man suffering with AIDS with a powerful testimony of God's grace in his life. We got along well together. Like all the counselors who worked one-on-one, he had come out of the gay scene. As well, he had received training in basic counseling techniques. More than just competent, Peter was empathetic, insightful, and able to fill the role of personal and spiritual mentor.

I continued going to Greenwood Gospel Chapel on Sundays and

gradually identified those who were in leadership. I was sure that I wanted to become part of their fellowship even before I was encouraged to do so by Peter. Yet I wasn't sure they would be quick to open the doors to me. I knew that social conservatism typically accompanied theological conservatism. Yet I felt comfortable with them for a variety of reasons. Several men from this church used to travel down to Trenton to speak at the Gospel Hall when I was a teenager. I myself had come to conferences here and met people who became lasting friends. This church was what I identified as "my tradition"; though I'd been away for a long time, these were my people.

A few weeks later, I spoke with Fred, one of the leaders who, I had learned, was a track coach who had worked with some big-name Canadian athletes as well as university-level runners. I introduced myself and broached the possibility of becoming part of the fellowship. I confessed that I hadn't been to church for a long time but affirmed that I felt comfortable with them and would like to meet with the leaders so we could become mutually better acquainted. He nodded in his characteristic way without looking me squarely in the eye and hurried away to consult with the others about setting up a time. When he returned, he said they would meet with me the following week after the service.

During the next few days, hope and insecurity wrestled for dominance. I spoke with Peter, who assured me this was a risk well worth taking. Yet twenty years in the gay scene had communicated clearly to me that most conservative Christians were uncomfortable with, if not contemptuous of, homosexuals. I kept thinking that if they turned me away, I could always try another church, but somehow, connecting with this particular group was important to me.

That next Sunday, I struggled to keep my mind on the service. It was a warm fall day in late September, and though the windows were open, I was perspiring as the service wrapped up and the elders made their way one by one to the lounge area. They pulled eight chairs into a circle, and we all sat there looking at each other, not knowing what to expect.

Fred began, "Gentlemen, this is Bob." We all nodded and smiled at each other as he continued. "You may have noticed him sitting at the back for the last few weeks. Bob tells me he hasn't been to a meeting for a long time, but he's thinking about asking for fellowship here." More nodding and smiling. "He asked to meet with us today so we can all get to know each other a little better." Then he turned and looked at me. "Why don't you tell us about who you are and why you're here?"

I looked around the circle of smiling faces. I hadn't seen anything like this for years. It was oddly comforting but uncomfortable at the same time. "I hardly know where to start, gentlemen," I began, "but it's probably best to begin with my childhood." And so I launched into a synopsis of the story of my life. I told them about the Baptist Sunday school, Youth for Christ, the Gospel Hall in Trenton, and conferences thirty years earlier in the building we were sitting in. Everyone kept nodding and smiling. Occasionally someone would offer a word of encouragement or comment on a name that I had mentioned.

When I finished rehearsing my spiritual life, I told them they'd only heard half the story. Now I wanted to go back and fill in the blanks. I told them about my family, particularly about my father. I mentioned Roger and my teenage sexual interest. The nodding and smiling faces became still and blank. Still I soldiered on. I told them about my divorce and my headlong involvement in the gay scene, not only in Toronto but in major American and European cities. Though the windows were still open, it seemed the air had stopped moving in the room.

When I finished all that, I told them about Sean's visit two months earlier and my desire to get out of the gay scene and my misgivings about being able to do that. I asked them if they would help me start over to make a new life for myself in their world. As I paused for breath at the end of all this, I wondered, *Will they, as a group of conservative, straight, evangelical Christians, open their hearts to me? Can I find a spiritual home among them?* Then I invited them to ask me any questions that came to their minds. I told them I would be one-hundred-percent truthful. I would not lie or hold anything back.

So the questions came. They did not turn the discussion into an inquisition, but they did have some legitimate concerns. Could I make any sort of guarantee I wouldn't attempt to have inappropriate relationships with the young men of the assembly? Was I sure I didn't have AIDS? How was I sure I didn't have AIDS? Would I be willing to spend what amounted to a probationary period with them during which we could get a sense of each other before being received into fellowship?

I must have responded to their concerns in a way that suited them, because once again heads started nodding and faces started smiling, though perhaps not quite as enthusiastically as at the beginning of the meeting. Gradually the air in the room started moving again, and by the time Fred asked Phil to wrap up our time in prayer, we all knew where things stood. When Phil finished praying he stood up, walked over to me, and put out his hand. "Bob, I want you to know we are with you all the way. We want to see you have the kind of life you're choosing to have now. Count on me to be there for you."

One by one, each of the men approached me and shook my hand. I suspect that if anyone had told them the day before that within twenty-four hours they'd be shaking hands with a gay man and offering to walk with him through the biggest challenge of his life, they would have thought it impossible. But they had done it. More than that, I had taken my first step toward a life that I had tasted but never truly embraced.

On my way home, I rejoiced as waves of delight and joy washed over me. These men had heard me out. They had accepted me. They believed that God could give me both forgiveness for my sins of the past and grace to make significant changes in the future. I couldn't wait until my next meeting with Peter to share the good news. That afternoon we laughed and cried together over the phone as we celebrated God's goodness to me.

25

Facing the Challenge

As the weather cooled that fall, my struggles were heating up. I spent a lot of time with my counselor, Peter, and with a couple of men from Greenwood, Fred and Phil. They became my first line of defense when I felt under attack, and they covered my back with moral and prayer support when I needed to move forward. The military metaphor suited my situation remarkably well, and as I embarked on this new, personal journey, I was aware that I had to deal with several "fronts" all at the same time.

My support group at the gay ministry was made up of eleven of us. We represented a variety of demographic groups. Among us were men and women, young and old. Most of us had been sexually active, but a couple of individuals had come primarily to face and deal with their feelings of same-sex attraction. Some of us were self-motivated and seeking help because we wanted it. Others had been sent by someone else, usually parents or a spouse. Most of us were single, but some were married. Many were dealing with abuse issues to one degree or another.

The two-hour sessions started with people telling their stories so we could get to know each other and start to open up channels of communication. We often learned as much from each other's experiences as we did from the evening's formal presentation. These covered same-sex-attraction issues, causes of homosexuality, the role of pornography, different manifestations of sexual variations like transvestism and transgenderism, masculinity, femininity, and a host of other related topics. Afterward, we'd discuss the material and talk about its application to our own situations.

I was one of those who sought out the program because I wanted to find a new direction for my life. I wanted to identify the factors that had contributed to my homosexuality and accept responsibility for my part so that I could move on with my life in a way that kept me in fellowship with God. I particularly wanted to be free of the addictive aspects of gay life. That scene had been such a part of my life for so long that I wasn't sure where the boundaries were. I longed for healthy, nonsexualized human relationships because I wanted to feel comfortable when I hugged my son or when a Christian brother put his arm across my shoulders when he prayed for me.

The hypersexualization of our culture makes developing godly patterns of relating very difficult. In the '60s, the worship of sex came out of the closet. Sex came to be seen as the greatest and highest good that offered humanity pleasure and power. We came to look to it for feelings of connectedness and transcendence. These are things that only God can truly give us, though I admit from my personal experience that unfettered sexual expression certainly gives a powerful illusion of those things.

Desexualizing my life involved changing the way I dressed, the places I went, the mannerisms I had adopted, my friendships, and—most significantly—my reorientation from adoring sexual experience to worshipping God. This single conscious shift in my thinking was the beginning of my new life. When sex ruled my life, my immediate urges got met, but there was no fundamental spiritual progress. I did not become a better man—a kinder, less selfish, more caring person. If anything, I became progressively more selfish and domineering.

I have to underline that while I made the decision to reorient my life, I certainly couldn't make the changes happen all on my own. This is the difference between serving the true God and any other things we set up as gods in our lives. They may grant us our immediate desires, but they cannot change us for the better. When I aligned myself with the living God, he began working in my life, and that has made all the difference.

At the same time, I soon found that sitting around waiting for a miracle was not an option. God was at work, to be sure, but I had to co-operate with him in the transformation process. The apostle Paul boldly stated, "If anyone is in Christ, he is a new creation; the old has gone, the new has come!" (2 Corinthians 5:17 NIV 1984). That sounds very absolute and I have no doubts about its validity as a truth statement. However, he also encouraged his readers to do as "you were taught, with regard to your former way of life, to put off your old self, which is being corrupted by its deceitful desires; to be made new in the attitude of your minds; and to put on the new self, created to be like God in true righteousness and holiness" (Ephesians 4:22–24). This makes clear the fact that we have "putting off" and "putting on" responsibilities in relation to the work God is doing in us.

I soon learned that my day-by-day response to God needed to be as intentional as my original decision to turn my focus from myself and my sexual desire to God and his holy purposes. That was a challenge. No, that *is* a challenge—because it requires looking at myself as objectively as possible and acknowledging my weaknesses. This was something I was never in the habit of doing. In fact, I avoided it. I was an in-control kind of guy. I did what I wanted, and I did it because I thought it was good for me. Acknowledging that some of my thinking, words, and behavior had a negative effect on both myself and others was foreign to me.

This kind of objective self-assessment was necessary for me to protect myself from exposure in the areas where I knew I was weak. Weaknesses are different for everyone. For example, pornography is a weakness for some of us. Knowing that allows me to avoid looking at anything that might head me into a binge. "Anything" could be something as inno-cent as the underwear section of a catalogue or a diving or wrestling

event on television. Regardless of how seemingly insignificant the thing
is that causes us to slip, we soon find ourselves sliding faster and faster,
until once again we are out of control.

The same is true of drug use. Just being in a place where I could catch
a whiff of pot used to be enough to head me toward a high, even though
I wasn't looking for it and perhaps was even mentally guarding against
it. Once the trigger releases the desire, there's almost no stopping it.
This principle is not just true of "big problems" like pornography, promiscuity, or drug use. It is equally applicable to people who shop, work,
or eat to deal with life. Which brings me to an important point.

Much, if not all, of our pursuit of negative behaviors—behaviors
harmful to ourselves or others—has nothing to do with the object of
our desire, whether it's sex, drugs, alcohol, food, work, or whatever.
We chase these things because we have a hole in our lives somewhere.
That hole might have been caused by a wound like childhood abuse
or neglect. Or it can result from a weak sense of identity or bad self-
perception, like "I'm stupid" or "I'm ugly."

From examining both what I was taught and my own life experience,
I discovered that my self-destructive way of living was a response to a
group of factors in my childhood and adolescence that were peculiar
to me. These things contributed to a hole in my life that I tried to fill
with gay sex and pot. Understanding the motivation for what I'd been
doing for the last twenty years led me to the inevitable conclusion that I
needed to fill that hole with something else. Unbeknownst to me, God
had already been working in my life to head me in the right direction. I
needed to let God himself heal my wounds and fill the big empty space
in my life.

After I completed the support-group program of the gay ministry,
I had a good grasp of the issues, how they interrelated, and how they
affected me personally. I was subsequently invited to join a growth
group which took us further, especially spiritually. At this stage we
talked much less about issues of homosexuality and focused instead
on steps toward spiritual maturity. The main thing that separated this

from other discipleship programs was that all of us had same-sex attraction as a common element in our backgrounds. Though this wasn't our focus, knowing that we had all wrestled with the same demons gave us a feeling of safety and allowed us to speak freely without fear of either offending or eliciting judgment from other group members.

As one would expect, the growth groups took the personal goals of their members into account. Most of us who continued to this second stage had experienced some kind of moral crisis in which we had come to the conclusion that homosexuality was wrong. Some guys were motivated by the fear of AIDS, but most of us were used to living with risk and were OK with that. Some found that their desire to be "normal"—to get married and have a family—was greater than their desire for same-sex relationships. For me, the goal was to develop spiritually.

This fit well with the stated purpose of the ministry at the time. The leadership team was convinced that if the group members were spiritually healthy, God's Spirit would work in us to accomplish his goals for us, and that was what really mattered. Some people went further than others in terms of change in their level of same-sex attraction, but most of us who went on to the growth groups did change profoundly in our relationship with God.

As for me, I came to think of myself not as "gay" or "ex-gay," just "free in Christ." Most heterosexual people don't think of themselves as "straight" or "not gay." They just live their lives. Christians, regardless of their sexual attraction, are free in Christ. Admittedly, the challenge is greater for gays not to think of themselves as gay, because a high percentage of gay life is about being gay in a sexual way. However, as we came to see life in a less sexualized way, it became easier for us to deepen our appreciation of our freedom in Christ, regardless of the particular sexual temptations we dealt with along the way.

Even after more than twenty years, one of the lessons I learned in those early days is still as applicable to my life now as it was then. I observed that the more I developed the spiritual side of my life, the easier it was to stay aligned with God's purposes for me. If I allowed gay sexual thoughts to settle in my mind, I would soon find myself struggling because what began as a foothold soon became a stronghold. Fulfilling the desires of the flesh always takes us away from God. When we live in the Spirit, we fulfill the desires of the Spirit.

Again I must emphasize my partnership with God in making the progress I have made in terms of sexual purity. As Christians, we would all like to have thoughts of Christ floating around in our minds as our default mental activity. I discovered that in order to have thoughts concerning Christ, I need to be thinking about Christ. In other words, the more I discipline my mind to think about the things in the Philippians 4:8 list (things that are true, noble, right, pure, lovely, admirable, excellent, or praiseworthy), the better my thoughts are.

This isn't trying to muster up feelings. It's choosing—making a conscious, intentional choice—to live out of the Spirit rather than living out of the flesh.

26

Witness

I'm the kind of person who throws himself one-hundred-percent into whatever he's doing. I certainly did it in the gay scene, and now that I was restored to the Lord, it was only natural that I live with the same devotion and intensity as I embraced a new life pattern. Week by week, I made gains as I refocused my attention and rechanneled my energy.

By the end of October 1991, my life was unrecognizable—even to me. Since Sean's visit at the end of July, I had experienced a spiritual awakening and plunged into church life at the chapel. I had begun withdrawing from the patterns of my gay life and filling the social void with new friendships. Best of all, I had a real relationship with God. I sensed his presence, and I knew he was changing me on the inside. Some changes had come quickly, others more gradually, but I was definitely in process.

With Peter's guidance and encouragement, I began to consciously shift my thinking from the track it had worn into a rut. This was the most difficult thing I had done in my life. My entry into the gay scene had been gradual and spontaneous. To leave it would have to be sudden and calculated. I faced the challenge of building a new social network of healthy, nonsexual relationships with both men and women as I cut ties with the men who had been my gay buddies.

Some of these guys had been mostly opportunistic in their relationships with me. Because of my jobs managing The Albany and working at The Diamond Club, I had solid contacts with several drug dealers. Though I never dealt myself, my friends all knew they could come to me to find out who had what at any given moment. Then there was the group of guys who had been sexual partners in the past. Lastly, there was a group of half a dozen guys whom I counted as friends. Of course they were gay; it was the only world I knew, and virtually all of the contacts I had came from within it. Yet I knew if I were going to maintain my resolve to go straight, I'd have to be honest with them, regardless of their response.

I phoned my inner circle of friends to tell them about my decision. I felt disappointment at how little my news affected them and sadness because of their total disinterest in hearing about the path on which I'd embarked. I wanted to talk to them about God and how Jesus had died to make it possible for me to have a new life. The most positive response I received came from Len. He told me he didn't mind if I talked to him about God, but he never wanted to hear anything about Jesus. When I tried to tell him that Jesus was the only way to know God, he cut me off. Cold.

Len's response surprised me because we both knew that he was not going to last more than a few months as he slowly lost the battle with AIDS. I guessed that since he'd lived his life without knowing Jesus, he was prepared to face eternity without him as well. We did agree on the fate of the sign-making business. He was happy to have me take it over completely; since I'd gotten involved, the cash flow had improved, so I was even able to pay him something for it to help cover what would be his final expenses.

During the last week of October that year, all of Toronto buzzed with the royal family's visit to the city. Prince Charles, Lady Diana, and Princes William and Harry grabbed headlines everywhere. The papers were full of pictures and stories about the royal visitors, but for the gay community, Lady Diana's visit to Casey House led them all. Everyone was grateful for her visit, because we hoped it would raise the profile of AIDS sufferers in the city. Fear flowed freely among both gays and straights. Men in the gay community often felt the rest of the world wanted to proceed as if their segment of society didn't exist. Far more than a gracious political gesture, Lady Diana's visit was the most practical help someone in her position could offer people with AIDS.

One Saturday evening I went out to pick up a few groceries and, while waiting in line, noticed a picture in the *Toronto Sun*. It showed Lady Diana at Casey House and there, with the best-known woman in the world, was my friend Wayne, sitting in a wheelchair with a quilt over his lap. I was shocked. It had only been a matter of months since we had been roommates, and here he was, under hospice care, his well-muscled body already wasting away. The complex of diseases that characterized the latter stages of AIDS was taking him down quickly.

Gratitude for having been spared overwhelmed me, followed immediately with grief at the thought of losing another friend. Now that I had begun experiencing a new freedom and sense of hope for myself, I wanted to share that with Wayne. Within a couple weeks, I went to visit him.

Casey House had been a grand old house, and it was set up to look somewhat like a small hotel with a central nurses' station and rooms off a corridor. The facility was clean and well maintained, but it was not pleasant because of the suffering and sorrow. It was impossible to mask the odors associated with terminal disease and death. Though the beginning of the disease was often asymptomatic, once the decline started, it was rapid. People looked wretched as they passed through the final stages. No wonder guys refused to be tested! They simply didn't want to know.

The areas for those in the final stages were kept dark because the light hurt their eyes. The atmosphere was very sad, and a nervousness about "catching it" made people guarded, as no one had clear answers about whether or not HIV could be transmitted through casual contact.

I paused at the nurses' station to inquire which room he was in. He was bedridden except for assisted trips to the bathroom. He looked frail, nothing like the powerful athlete he'd been. The legs that had once propelled him around the ball diamond were thin and limp. The arms that could blast a ball out of the park were emaciated and weak.

When I approached his bed, he turned his head and his face lit up. He introduced me to another visitor who had arrived earlier. I knew I needed to see him alone if we were to have a serious talk. Only then would we both feel free enough to open up about things many gay guys suppress. So the three of us chatted about baseball, especially the good fortunes of the Blue Jays that year, until it became clear to me his other friend intended to stay for a long while yet. I excused myself and went back to the apartment and prayed for another chance.

The next week I made another visit and found the same man visiting Wayne. I struggled to register the speed at which my friend was deteriorating. He had lost more weight, and his skin had taken on the blotchy discolorations we saw so often in late-stage AIDS. This time the friend and I did most of the talking. The attendants were giving Wayne morphine for pain, and he drifted in and out without being able to contribute much to the conversation. I felt hopeless. Even if I were alone with him, he was so doped up I wasn't sure he'd be able to understand anything. Again I said good-bye and silently prayed it wouldn't be my last farewell.

The next week, things were even worse. He was skeletal and the patches of discoloration were now so large they were meeting along their edges. This time, the other visitor left first, but again my desire to share my newfound hope with Wayne was thwarted because he was sleeping soundly and oblivious to everything around him. My heart ached for him. I loved this man, not just because of our previous intimate relationship but because we were friends. We had sat across the table from each other countless times, eating and laughing together. We had shared the thrill of victory and had commiserated with each other over our defeats on the ball diamond.

I left his room and tracked down a nurse. I told her I had to talk to

Wayne at least one more time and pressed her to tell me about his ~~cation~~ schedule.

"He gets his afternoon meds at two o'clock," she said. "If you want a chance to talk with him when he's coherent, the best time would be about one thirty, when the effects of the previous dose will be wearing off."

Grateful for this inside information I walked back to the apartment, praying God would give me a chance to talk to Wayne alone when he was conscious enough to understand.

The next week as I approached Wayne's room, it was extraordinarily quiet. I peeked in and saw Wayne by himself. The clock at the foot of his bed read 1:35. This was my chance. He heard me close the door and followed me with his eyes as I pulled a chair close to the bed, reached out, and took his hand. Too weak to move his head, he gave my hand a tiny squeeze when I greeted him.

Asking him how he was doing was pointless. He had pneumonia and his chest was filling up. He couldn't speak. In fact, he couldn't do much of anything. I leaned toward him, and with my lips only a handbreadth or so from his ear, I spoke softly. "Wayne, it makes me sad to see you like this, but I'm glad I can talk to you for a few minutes."

His eyes were closed and his breathing could best be described as ragged. "Wayne, you know and I know that you're getting near the end of the time you have here."

I paused, searching for the strength to say what I wanted to say.

"You need to know something else. This isn't just the end; it's also a beginning. In spite of how well we've known each other, you don't know something that has happened to me in the last couple of months."

I knew this would be my only chance to talk to him and I struggled to keep my emotions under control.

"Wayne, you know what a selfish guy I've been. I've hurt a lot of people by taking what I could get without caring much about them. I've hurt you, Wayne. I know that. I also know that selfishness has another name. It's sin. It's called that because it hurts people and offends God.

I'd love to be able to tell you that you don't need to worry about this, because you're such a great guy, but let's be honest here. We know we're both selfish. We know we've both hurt other people and offended God."

Sink or swim: I was in over my head and treading water for all I was worth. Punctuating every sentence with a silent prayer, "God help me," I told him what I'd learned as a child and forgotten as an adult—that love and forgiveness were not just a dream. Though I'd intentionally turned my back on them, I'd been confronted by the truth and stepped into the reality of spiritual life.

"Wayne, I want you to know that in spite of everything in your life that has been selfish and sinful and wrong, you can have forgiveness. If you accept Jesus's death on the cross as the payment for your sin, God does the same thing. Your body will die, of course. It can't last much longer. But your spirit will live on in the presence of God, forever."

I leaned back and sighed, having said all I wanted to say. Well, *almost* all. I leaned back close to his ear.

"Wayne, this is an important time. I know you can't speak to me, but you can squeeze my hand. If you're trusting God to receive you when you leave your body, because you believe Jesus died for your sin, then squeeze my hand."

I finished speaking and I felt his fingers stir in my palm. He squeezed my hand for several seconds, using up as much energy as he could spare from the important business of keeping his diaphragm moving up and down. As his fingers relaxed in my hand, I burst into tears. I had just witnessed a dear friend leave the darkness behind and step into the light. I sat there, staring at his face, gaunt and discolored almost beyond recognition, yet somehow glowing with the presence of Jesus. It was the most powerful experience I'd ever had, and I savored the moment as long as I could.

Then a thought hit me. "One more thing, old friend," I whispered. "A few weeks ago, you met Lady Di. We all saw the picture in the paper. She came here and talked to you. I'll bet it was the best thing that ever happened to a guy in Casey House. You were in the presence of royalty. But, Wayne, that pales beside what happened in this room today. Jesus came and met you here. He welcomed you into his family." Again Wayne's fingers fluttered in my palm. Indeed, we had both been in the presence of Royalty.

I don't remember how long I stayed with him, holding his hand and gazing at his face, but the nurse startled me when she came in with his morphine. "I'm putting some more morphine into your IV, sweetie," she said to him. "We'll keep you as comfortable as we can." She smiled sadly at me. "There's nothing more to do at this point."

"Everything that can be done has been done," I agreed.

The next day, I called Casey House to see how Wayne was. The nurse told me he had passed away peacefully in the early hours of the morning. I smiled my own sad little smile as I thought to myself, *He knew he had a place to go to. It was finally safe to go home.*

27

Following Through

Fred and his wife, Mary, took a deep personal interest in me. They often invited me around for meals, and I found I could be totally open about my past with them. One thing I appreciated most about Fred was that he was not in the least naive about the gay scene, unlike some of the other elders who had a more sheltered existence. This allowed me to speak very directly to him about my journey and to verbalize my thoughts in a way that brought clarity, not just to him but to me as well.

One Sunday afternoon, after a wonderful meal, Mary disappeared from the scene and left Fred and me to chat. Never one to beat around the bush, he began asking me about how I was doing. I could tell by the way he asked his questions that he had some expectation that I must be wrestling with strong sexual temptations.

I explained that I had learned it's one thing to make a decision but something else entirely to implement it. During Sean's visit, I became aware of my dissatisfaction with what I had been pursuing as a gay man, so it wasn't difficult to decide to abandon it and move forward with my life on another track.

Fred probed a little deeper. A true spiritual shepherd, he needed to know what was going on in the life of his people if he were to be able to help them in a meaningful way. Knowing this, I couldn't resent his pointed questions and did my best to answer.

"Listen, Fred, I'd be lying if I told you that I never had a homoerotic fantasy, lustful thought, or even an outright temptation."

He nodded to indicate that he thought as much. "So how are you dealing with those things, Bob?"

I went on to explain some things I'd been thinking as Peter and I worked our way through the different aspects of my decision and its ramifications. I told Fred that I'd learned that all people are only tempted in areas where they have desire. The same thief who is quick to steal your laptop from your car may well leave behind the suit that you just picked up from the dry cleaner, even though it may be worth more. The same glutton who might consume a box of doughnuts for breakfast may turn up his nose at a generous helping of porridge.

I explained that I was in the process of intentionally cultivating new, healthy desires that met my needs without setting me up for addictive responses, whether to substances, behaviors, or particular kinds of relationships. This was crucial for me. Reordering my desires changed everything, because almost everything we do starts out as a desire.

Since Fred was well acquainted with the Bible, I made an oblique reference to James 1:15. I like to think of desire as a fertilized egg in a pregnant woman. Just as a woman unwittingly nourishes and nurtures the growing baby until birth, so we feed and protect our desire until it matures and is born into the world in the form of actions. Those actions may be wise or foolish, constructive or destructive, good or bad, and so on. Once our actions are set in motion, they head toward an eventual end, either of personal wholeness, social benefit, and capital-L Life, or of personal loss, social detriment, and eventual spiritual death. While I didn't consciously choose same-sex attraction and activity to meet my deepest needs, I learned that *I could* choose other desires and behaviors to fulfill those same goals.

Fred told me he liked the way I had explained how I was working things through for myself and asked me to tell him more, if I were comfortable doing that. I assured him I was and explained that through my sexual experiences, beginning with Roger and then moving on through liaisons with other men, I had developed a taste for some particular homosexual activities as a way of meeting my need to feel masculine, to belong, to know who I was. This was something I learned. The decision I made about leaving the gay scene wasn't just about sex and sexuality. It centered on where I would get my identity and what I would use to feed my psychological needs of connection, fulfillment, transcendence, and so on. When homosexual thoughts passed through my mind—and they often did for quite a while—I reminded myself that I had chosen a different way to meet my deepest psychological needs.

I went on to explain that I refused to allow my mind to linger on sexual memories of the past. I chose to refocus my attention on my new desires to be whole, to be free of addictions, to identify myself as a man made in the image of the Divine (not specifically as a gay man or a straight man); and I chose to look to God and my relationship with him and fellowship with his people to give me all the psychological benefits I had looked for in gay relationships.

That long conversation with Fred cemented our relationship, and I knew I could count on him to rejoice with me in my victories and support me in my weakness.

Fred and Mary were just two of many people at Greenwood who not only took an interest in me and my well-being but also contributed directly to my spiritual development. I soon made friends with Greg, a godly young man. We clicked right away, and it wasn't long before I shared my story with him. I couldn't help wondering how his having that information about me would affect the way he responded to me, and I was greatly relieved when I discerned no difference at all. I continue to enjoy his full acceptance of me as a brother in Christ.

One of the many positive things about Greg was his self-confidence. He knew exactly who he was and wasn't trying to prove anything in his relationships. This allowed me to be comfortable and to gain confidence in myself, even as I grew more secure in this healthy man-to-man relationship. As we got to know each other better, he began to share with me some of his own challenges, and we decided to meet occasionally for early-morning prayer times. These allowed us to support each other in our particular personal and spiritual challenges and to deepen our relationship with each other and with the Lord. These continued on and off until a move took him to another part of the province.

During the winter of 1991–92, I learned that two of the Greenwood women met weekly for prayer focused on the church family and those near and dear to them. Clara and Anna represented a challenge to me because I had not had a normal friendship with a woman for many years. For the most part, the only female friends I had were lesbians, and I didn't suppose that those friendships were representative of the way most opposite-sex adults related to each other. Clara and Anna were a few years younger than me, but spiritually they were far more mature.

I began by speaking to them at meetings, particularly with Clara, who was the more outgoing of the two. They weren't bashful about their prayer times, and inevitably, during one of our friendly chats over coffee in the chapel basement, Clara asked me if I had anything for Anna and her to pray about when they got together the following Friday evening. I responded quickly with a couple of concerns about my growing business and my spiritual life. Then I followed with a few questions about their prayer meetings.

"Are they really 'meetings,'" I asked, "or just the two of you getting together to pray?"

"Well," Clara explained, "so far, it's just the two of us, but we're open to others joining us, so I guess that's why I think of them as prayer meetings."

"Is this a women-only kind of thing, or could a guy join you?"

Clara was enthusiastic. "We'd be glad to have a man come along. Are you fishing for a personal invitation?"

"Well, I was kind of wondering if I'd be welcome or not. I'd like to get to know the people in the fellowship better and thought that praying for them with you and Anna might be a good way to do that."

She told me that Anna was coming to her house that week and they'd gladly welcome me.

That connection was important to me for several reasons. It set me on the road to having normal, healthy, nonsexual relationships with women. It plugged me into the inner workings of the fellowship, its people, and their needs. And it was personally gratifying as, opening their hearts to me, Anna and Clara made me feel like part of their little prayer team. Eventually, because of their acceptance and warmth, I decided to share some of my story with them. I figured it would be a good way to get a sense of how others in the chapel might respond, should I decide to tell them or in case they found out some other way.

Once again I was pleasantly surprised. They accepted the news as a simple fact and didn't exhibit a big, emotional reaction. Since we had been praying together, they took advantage of the opportunity to pray for me, thanking God for what he had done and was doing in my life. I continued to meet with them, and due to our ongoing friendship, I encouraged myself with the thought that if word got out about me, it wouldn't be the end of the world—not even the end of my fellowship with the Christians at Greenwood Gospel Chapel.

28

The Purge

Writing is a linear activity; living is not. Inevitably, things were happening all at once. One of the early lessons I learned through the gay ministry was the need to purge the physical reminders of my former way of living. This would remove at least some of the triggers that in the past had consistently led to activities I was conscientiously trying to avoid. This was made blessedly easy by the fact that at the very time this came up, I was in the process of packing up the apartment to move to my new house on Broadview Avenue.

The move certainly didn't isolate me from all the gay men I knew, but it distanced me from the gay village and its constant reminders of my old life. Within weeks, most of the friendships I'd had with other gay men evaporated as I told them about my decision to change the direction of my life. I didn't separate myself from my gay friends so much as they separated themselves from me. It was our same-sex attraction and activity that provided the bond for us, and when that was gone I was no longer "one of them." They weren't mean or even unkind, just suddenly disinterested. Speaking generally, they weren't expressing an anti-Christian bias through this, though a few did. Mostly it was a simple matter of no longer having in common the one thing that brought us together.

My old friends were so committed to their life in the world of same-sex attraction that they didn't want to hear anything that might suggest they should change. They were in it because they wanted to be in it, just as I had been until I realized that I didn't want to be in it anymore. I accepted the loss of these friendships with mixed emotions. On the one hand, I was saddened by the fact that these men with whom I had worked, played, lived, and been intimate didn't want to carry on their friendships with me; on the other hand, I knew that the old patterns were strong and would be a constant pull back into the world I was leaving. Even so, I depended on the fact that "the one who is in [me] is greater than the one who is in the world" (1 John 4:4).

Real faith led to real change in my life. As I packed my belongings, I sorted them into boxes to go with me and garbage bags to go into the dumpster. I easily decided the fate for most things. All of my dirty movies went into garbage bags. I had used them to create the right mood when I had guys over to the apartment for sex. No need for them anymore. I didn't have a lot of printed porn—I had preferred to be out on the hunt rather than sitting home alone looking at pictures—but what I had joined the movies in the trash.

When it came to my photo albums, I struggled a bit. I had done a lot of traveling and had pictures from all over the world. I valued them. At the same time, I had lots of pictures which my former partners had given me, and others we'd taken on outings to places like the gay beach on Centre Island. I compromised by going through them all and pulling out all of the pictures of the men I'd been with. I didn't need to be reminded of them. I had enough problems with my memory as it was, and it didn't need refreshing every time I flipped through my pictures.

This issue of memories bears commenting on. When we engage in activities, especially when there is a lot of emotional content, we remember them. Sexual encounters tend to be highly charged, exciting moments, and details are burned into the memory circuits of our brains in a way that almost nothing else is. I have many memories I wish I could forget, and even with the passing of time they remain uncomfortably sharp. What's more, they pop into my head at the most inopportune times, like when I'm attempting to pray or worship.

Often something I see in my environment will trigger a memory, so I'm careful not to put myself in situations where I might see things that would lead me to think about my old life and the men who were part of it. This means deciding to turn off the TV sometimes. When I do encounter same-sex attraction expressed on the street or on a TV program, it doesn't shock me, but I feel sad. Sad because I know it displeases the Lord, and sad because of the memories it triggers in me of the twenty years of my life that I'll never get back.

One item was a particular challenge. I came across my little brass toke box hidden away among some other once-treasured possessions and wondered what to do with it. In a strange way, I valued it. It was my first toke box in Toronto so far as I knew. I had picked it up, along with several others, on a trip to Chicago and had introduced them to some of the head shops on Yonge Street, where they soon became hot items. In a matter of weeks, I saw more and more of them showing up around the city. This particular toke box had been my constant companion for years and had a certain amount of sentimental value. At the same time, I didn't want to keep it because I was purging everything to do with my old life, and this certainly was a significant part of that. Neither did I want to give it to anyone I knew because that could be seen as encouraging them to smoke up, and I didn't want to do that. Eventually I decided to put it in the garbage.

Overall, the purge process wasn't difficult for me, especially at the time when I did it. I was still in the first blush of enthusiasm for my new life. Occasionally I remember something I threw away during that brief period of my life, but I've never been sorry for shutting the door on physical things that could have been sources of temptation.

Of course, simply disposing of the negative in our lives is not enough. If we are going to experience beneficial life change, we have to focus on the positive. While accountability groups can be helpful if they are conducted well, they can also be harmful if they keep everyone focused on the problem instead of the solution. Any success I have experienced in changing my life has resulted from concentrating on filling my life with the good things I wanted, not just trying to get rid of what I no longer valued.

Early in my new life I began to discover replacements for my frenetic activity in the gay community. The first developed as a natural consequence of my associating with a healthy local church where the people were truly friends. This was demonstrated by their love of socializing. Suddenly I was being invited to meals, especially Sunday dinners, and other fellowship occasions—often on Sunday evenings after the service. Because of these opportunities to get to know other people on a personal level, friendships began to grow like the ones with Greg, Clara, Anna, Fred and Mary, and lots of others.

While we enjoyed conversation about a wide range of topics, we often discussed sermons we'd heard or passages from the Bible we'd read on our own. This prompted me to use some of my time alone in Bible study—something I used to love doing in my older teenage years and felt comfortable getting back into. I enjoyed the challenge of understanding not just specific details of the Word but also its big-picture concepts, which enriched my understanding of the details.

This had an important impact on me. Paul wrote about the purifying effect of the Word of God in the life of the church in general and individual believers in particular. He spoke of the Lord sanctifying and cleansing the church "by the washing with water through the word" (Ephesians 5:26). I found my extended times of Bible reading and study to be helpful in refocusing my attention from the physical world around me to the spiritual realm, which, I discovered, was also around me and just as real as the physical. As I nurtured my spirit, my intense desire to gratify my flesh began to fade.

In the interest of honesty, though, I confess this wasn't a "miracle." At times I had to discipline my mind both to choose what conformed to my new great desire in life—to be the man God intended me to be— and to focus my attention on whatever spiritual theme I was studying at the time. If we all did what we were supposed to do simply because it was the right thing, the world would be a very different place. But the fact is, we often fail to do the *right* thing because it is also often the *difficult* thing. Also in the interest of honesty, I have to say that what was happening in my life was beyond what I could have done on my own. God was clearly at work as I attempted to cooperate with him.

One of the practical ways the change in me came to my attention was in my relationships. I'd developed the unhealthy habit of focusing on people's physical attributes, especially with men. Evaluating them sexually was so ingrained in me that it was "just the way I was." Yet as I grew in my relationship with the Lord, I found my emphasis shifting from having a sexual interest in people to having a personal interest in them. Clearly this was something I worked on consciously, but I know also that this development was not something I could have made happen out of my own strength.

29

Processing

I had never been a particularly thoughtful person. I was ruled by my basic appetites for food, drink, sleep, and sex. Once I decided to follow Jesus, this had to change. The change was facilitated in part by my ability to reflect on what was happening in and around me and process it in a way that made sense, given my new approach to life.

Looking back from the vantage point of several months of living by faith, I was somewhat unsettled to think I was so ignorant about sex and sexuality that when Roger molested me as a boy, I really didn't know what was happening. Even more amazing to me now was that I'd had no moral misgivings about my activities.

I was so naive, so undisciplined, so unsupervised, so emotionally vulnerable, and so ill-taught that I guess I shouldn't have been surprised. Without any moral voice in my life offering direction, once same-sex attraction manifested in my relationship with Roger, I headed down a path I believe I could have stopped much more easily in those early days but had no motivation to do so.

That first sexual experience was so powerful that the context became the pattern for me. I learned later that some same-sex-attracted people never act out; they just feel the attraction and either ignore or accept it. Others stay closeted and have very limited sexual encounters, living a double life and working hard to maintain the separation. Still others follow the social patterns of the majority, get married, and act out only occasionally.

Finally, there is an increasingly large group, of which I was a part, that goes through every door that opens. They end up being promiscuous and, in some ways, the stereotypical "gay" envisioned by the straight world, though in fact, gays come in as many varieties as heterosexual people do, and gay lifestyles are as diverse as straight ones, ranging from celibate to promiscuous.

I accepted that my gayness developed over time. Doing so freed me from the pressure of expecting my desires to stop immediately; in fact, it took years of waiting on the Lord before I regularly got a good night's sleep without fantasies, memories, sexual dreams, and nocturnal emissions. Giving myself time was a grace that I believe God himself gave to me.

Being a Christian made a huge difference in the process I had undertaken. I went from fully accepting my homosexual behaviors to recognizing that, however the same-sex attraction started, the activities were against God's design for humanity. From there it was a matter of translating what I believed into the way I lived my life. This is why I believe Sean's visit was so important. It provided the catalyst to push me into this final stage.

As I came to grips with what the Bible says about homosexuality, I had to accept that regardless of the factors that had led me into this activity, I was responsible for the choices that kept me there and moved me deeper and deeper into dependence on it. I admitted to myself that my conscience had started nagging me about it years ago. The weekend when Steve called me a hypocrite demonstrated that even back in my gay heyday, I had some moral reservations about what I was doing, though it was never enough to make me give it up.

Once I accepted *that*, I had to take responsibility for my choices and then take action to change my behavior. I got a lot of help with this from the ministry to gays. The support groups and one-on-one sessions with Peter helped me accept the role so many others had played in my life that contributed to my ending up where I had. At the same time, I had to admit that none of them, not even Roger, had acted with the intent of bringing me to the place I had been.

It is easy to excuse oneself by blaming others. But when I did that, I gave them all the power. How could I change if others had done this to me? It was only after I recognized my personal decision-making power that I was able to take control of my life and begin reversing the choices I, not others, had made. I could never change the things that happened to me, but I didn't have to go on accepting their power over me.

I determined to commit my way to the Lord, trusting him to bring it to pass (Psalm 37:5). I sensed that if I didn't resolve to align myself with God's purposes and change the patterns of my life, I would remain vulnerable indefinitely—the one thing I didn't want. I chose to consciously cooperate with God, to forget my old life and the patterns that had such a hold on me, as I reached out to grasp the high calling of God on my life (Philippians 3:12–14).

Even as I gained insights from God's Word, I learned things from my own experience. For example, I found I could not control the thoughts that drifted into my mind. Over the years, we develop habits of thinking just as surely as we develop habits of acting. For twenty years I had indulged my thought life with homoerotic fantasies. And I can witness to the fact that what a man thinks in his heart is what he does (Proverbs 4:23) because I found guys to live out those fantasies with me. My mind imagined things, my will determined to do them, and I found ways and people with whom to make them happen. Now I had to train my mind to reject those fantasies and replace them with pure thoughts that honored God and built me up spiritually.

Well, you say, that's got to be a tough assignment. Maybe even impossible. I agree, at least with the first part. It *is* a tough assignment. But it's not impossible. When a Christian faces a major challenge, the first thing he does is pray, so I prayed. But I quickly found that prayer is not some magical cure. It helped, but focusing on my problem *was* part of the problem. Early on I discovered that some prayer activity actually got me obsessing about my troubles, whatever they might have been at the moment.

For a long time, when I went to bed, I'd be afraid to go to sleep because as soon as I did, I'd be back in the bathhouse in my dreams. This distressed me deeply. When I was conscious and an unwholesome thought came to mind, I could take intentional action and redirect my mind elsewhere. But when I was asleep, my dreams ran their course. I would often wake up feeling defiled by what had just happened, though it was out of my control.

I tried all kinds of things to help. Some were of limited benefit; most were of none. But I didn't give up, and while victory didn't come quickly or easily, by the grace of God, it came. For me, the biggest single step toward that victory was an obvious one, though I had overlooked it. For ten to fifteen minutes before I went to bed, I'd read a psalm or some other portion of the Bible that focused my attention on the Lord, his greatness, and what he had done for me. Then I'd have a little prayer time and finish off by intentionally thinking about what I'd read as I was drifting off to sleep.

The difference was like night and day in terms of freedom from the sexual thoughts that oppressed me. As I write this, I can honestly say I haven't had a sexual dream for several years. I won't pretend that I never have sexual thoughts, but they are infrequent and hardly bother me because I know how to reduce their impact, if not entirely get rid of them.

As I matured, I was invited to lead a support group for gay men and, later, a growth group. One of the things I stressed to the fellows was that as long as we're in the flesh, we'll never arrive. Even Paul said that the things he wanted to do, he didn't do, and the things that he didn't want to do, he did (Romans 7:15). I urged them to never excuse their sin, but at the same time to recognize that they are in process. Wars are won battle by battle, often on different fronts at the same time. It's tough, but while we're weak and fickle, the Lord is strong and faithful. His sufficient grace is always available.

Now, as I share my story, I can tell people that I find great refreshment in my spiritual life which takes priority over my physical comfort and pleasure. The key to it all has been the development of a deep desire for the things of God. I have a conscious and intentional desire for God that transcends desires for physical and sexual pleasure. When sexually tempting thoughts come to mind, I remind myself that this is not what I have chosen to bring meaning to my life, and I refocus on what I want to be and what God wants to do in me.

Sometimes people ask me if gay men like me can leave the gay scene behind without becoming a Christian. I tell them that it is theoretically possible if the desire is great enough, but I know that for me it would not have been possible. Without that deep desire to know God, I could never have succeeded in changing my behavior. We are always going to satisfy our desires; that's how we're designed. The secret to success is to have the right desires. Then the drive to satisfy the desires will take us in the right direction.

We all reinforce our perceptions, values, and attitudes through repetition. Just as athletes and musicians develop their physical muscles through repetition to such a degree that they can respond to stimuli without conscious thought, our ways of thinking are similarly strengthened.

Many specific aspects of homosexuality are reinforced through repetition. Every time we engage in thoughts and actions, we build reflex responses about which we no longer think consciously. I have seen those areas in my own life lose their grip on me when I treated them like an addiction. People say things like, "I eat because I'm bored," or "I drink because I'm lonely," or "I do drugs because I'm anxious," or "I do extreme sports because it gives me a feeling of power." I used sexual encounters to make myself feel accepted, powerful, worthy, free, and special. I needed sex to feel loved.

Regardless of what our stumbling blocks might be—sex, alcohol, drugs, food, or whatever—the drive to indulge is less about the substance or the behavior itself and much more about the psychological need that drives it. Eventually, I got to the point where I realized that the sex, cigarettes, and pot that I thought I was using were, in fact, using me. It was then that I decided to find other physically healthier ways of coping with my psychological needs. I suspect that others may also find this to be true in their lives.

Some people would argue with me, especially those whose desire is still what we might call low grade—that is, it does what they want it to do without interfering significantly with other aspects of their lives. They would say that the habitual use of a substance or other behavioral pattern is not an overwhelming force at all. I believe that is a matter of semantics. It doesn't mean that they are not "dependent" on whatever it is they crave. People often don't recognize their dependence on what they've chosen to satisfy their needs because, at some level, whatever it is they are using works for them. Only when it interferes with other aspects of their life do they become willing to see it as the problem it is.

For years I lived addicted to substances and behaviors that were slowly building a web of control over my life, my way of thinking, my manner of speech, and my behavior. At what point did I cross the line from using these things to being addicted to them? I have no idea. What I do know is that when I treated my addictions as being what they were and took steps to remove them from my life, they responded to the treatment.

Now, more than twenty years down the road, I still think about the issues. I don't obsess about them, but from time to time I roll them over in my mind as I seek to understand more of what God has done in my life and help others discover what he wants to do in theirs.

30

Reaching Out

Few people leaving the LGBT community are able to do so without structured support. I found this to be true in my case, so the invitation from the gay-ministry leadership team for me to move into roles that allowed me to build into the lives of others pleased me. The support groups I led featured the same mix of people and motives I had observed when I came looking for help: men and women, young and mature, shy and outgoing, willing and reluctant participants, and so on. The variety of personalities and experiences enriched the interactions.

The meetings were held in the second-floor lounge of the Christian-education wing of a large downtown church. The south-facing windows let in the maximum amount of light regardless of the season of the year and gave us a view over the busy street below. It was a warm, welcoming environment with couches and coffee tables, which helped people feel at ease—an important asset for those who were being asked to open up about the most intimate aspect of their lives.

On one occasion, as we settled into our places and people chatted with their neighbors, a slim man with dark hair, appearing to be in his mid to late thirties, made his way into the circle and sat down. As I watched him introduce himself to the people next to him, I sensed that he would be one of the willing participants.

I introduced myself and welcomed everyone, expressing my hope that they would feel comfortable to share and assuring them that there was no pressure to do so. This was important because I knew that some of those gathered may not have been there entirely voluntarily. As we went around the circle introducing ourselves, we came to the man I had noticed earlier. My initial assessment of him proved accurate. He told us his name was Frank, and he thanked the group for making a place for him. Then, as the others had done before him, he gave us a condensed version of his story.

Frank had grown up in a family that was already comfortable with homosexuality. Three of his uncles were out and accepted. Frank's same-sex interest began when, as a boy of four, some older boys, including one of his uncles, invited him to join them in some mutual sexual experimentation. By the time he was in high school, he considered himself gay. He'd had a string of relationships and, for a time, supported himself by offering sexual services for money. During this period, he met a street chaplain who introduced him to a church where he had met Jesus. One thing led to another, and now he was with us seeking support to leave the same-sex world behind.

We continued on around the circle, and once we all knew each other by name, I explained the purpose of the support group and our expectations of its members. Everyone bought into the program and was grateful for the benefits they could already see, but none as enthusiastically as Frank.

Over the course of the next few weeks I learned more of the details of Frank's life. My interest in his story was piqued by some of the differences between it and my own, particularly in regard to his relationship with his father. Frank had never had a coming-out conversation with his parents. He simply lived out his choices in front of them. His father was always accepting of everything he did. Frank's place in the family as a beloved son was never in doubt. He always spoke highly of his dad, who, Frank liked to say, "loved me and never failed to show it."

With that early acceptance in his family, especially by his father,

Frank was open and fearless and described himself as "a bit of an activist." After finishing his education, he lived with a partner, got a good job, and began living the life. To many gay guys this might sound pretty idyllic, but Frank wasn't entirely happy. Indeed, he soon came to see himself as unsatisfied and unhappy.

I remember an occasion when Frank had the floor in one of our support-group sessions. "The problem wasn't that I was gay," he said. "I was unhappy because I had become a sex addict. At first I thought domestic gay life was what I wanted, but I wasn't satisfied. Within a week of moving in with my partner, I discovered that one partner wasn't nearly enough."

People in the circle nodded in sympathy. Many of us knew exactly what he was talking about. Frank continued, "So I concluded I needed to make a change. I moved on to another relationship. Again, it was exciting at first, but I soon found weaknesses in the new arrangement, and I pushed on.

"It wasn't long before I identified this as a pattern in my life. I always felt that there was something missing. A new relationship would make me feel complete for a while, but then the glow would fade and I'd find myself looking around again. I never had enough." Frank paused and looked around the circle for encouragement. "Whether it was work, or money, or sexual encounters, I was never satisfied with what I had for more than a few weeks at a time.

"In my search, I got involved with a group from California that blended aspects of Eastern mysticism with sexual activity, and I learned both spiritual and sexual techniques from them. I thought that maybe getting plugged into the spiritual realm would help fulfill me. I even became partners with one of the leaders of the group and began arranging workshops which we led together. We were trying to help men strengthen their spiritual and sexual energy."

Frank paused for effect and again looked around the group, this time to make sure everyone was listening. We were. "That only lasted for a while, and then I started looking for something else."

I always watched the group carefully at times like this. As usual, slowly nodding heads showed sympathy and wry faces indicated that people were identifying strongly.

Frank continued, "I connected with a couple of hippies who had bought fifty acres north of the city. They were going to build a grassroots community far from the hustle and bustle of life in the big city. This got me thinking: *Why am I going to work? Why am I living in the city? Why do I put up with the constant cycle of construction and destruction around me?*

"I didn't have a good answer to those questions, so I began to prepare to join my new friends. The plan was to simplify our lives and find happiness close to nature, working the earth, planting seeds, tending crops, and eating the things we grew. I threw my heart into the scheme in its earliest days. I quit my job in the air-conditioning business to free up my time. Of course, this meant I didn't have money for my nice apartment and had to give it up as well.

"The place up north wasn't ready to live in, so I rented a room in The Beaches. Of course I needed some money for that, so I started to offer a particular form of massage in a walk-up room at the back of an apartment over a bakery near where I lived." He looked around, assessing whether or not we'd picked up the inference. "This is putting it politely. In fact, I was making my living by prostituting myself. I'd be working around home, cooking or something, and I'd get a call from a client. I'd arrange to meet him and whisk him up the stairs to this rented room, where I'd take care of him. It was a great little arrangement for me."

Frank went on to tell us how Al, the street chaplain, connected with him. You wouldn't think that a gay prostitute and a chaplain, even a street chaplain, would have much in common, but it turned out they did. "I often had free time during the day and liked to cook. Al was often available during the day and liked to eat. So we began spending a fair bit of time together." Smiles went around the group as they considered the incongruity of the friendship. Even though we were meeting in facilities belonging to a church, many of the LGBT community, even some in the support group, had experienced rejection from Christians.

"Because I enjoyed stirring things up," Frank continued, "I didn't hide anything from him. I told him about my partner in San Francisco and our plans for him to come to Canada. I told him about my goal to live up north with my friends, mostly because I liked to talk about what we did every weekend I could manage to get there. I didn't have to tell him about what I did for a living because I had ads in the papers and he saw them. I sometimes brought our chats to a sudden end when a client would call and I'd have to ditch Al to take care of the client.

"Because Al was patient and listened to me, I felt I had to return the favor, so I listened to him share things about his life and talk about church and his Christian friends as naturally as I talked about my life. Eventually he got around to inviting me to come to church with him. I assured him that I wanted nothing to do with his church. But eventually, in an effort to get him to shut up about it, I agreed to go to a meeting with him one Sunday evening, though I had absolutely no desire to go."

"You must have been desperate to get him off your case," said Dave, a member of the group who frequently remarked that he didn't like meeting in a Baptist church.

"But it wasn't as bad as I thought it would be," Frank said. "For one thing, they met in an office building I was familiar with because I had helped put the cooling system in it. Secondly, the preacher, who wore ordinary clothes—no robes—was a really good speaker. I have a lot of respect for people who can speak well in front of people, because I know how difficult it is to stand up and be articulate. On top of this, the worship leader was a young, good-looking guy." Frank paused and waited for the snickers to subside.

"Suddenly church didn't seem as bad as I thought it would be. I decided to go back. I'll admit that having that young worship leader to look at played a role in my wanting to do that, but I had another motive. Without realizing it, I had put myself in a place where I would hear the gospel over and over.

"So I kept going back and met more people and made friends with some. I got to meet the pastor and started going to the college-and-career group as well as something called the 'school of discovery,' which introduced people to the church. It was a place for skeptics and unbelievers like me to ask questions and find answers. Personally, I never had a problem with Jesus. My beef was with God. If he really was who he seemed to be saying he was, why did everything in the world look like it was out of control?

"I was also pretty sure that if Jesus were living in Toronto in our generation, he'd be in Allen Gardens with the drug addicts and the homeless, not serving Mass at the cathedral down the street. Sure enough, the more I learned about Jesus, the more convinced I was that I was right about that, and the better I liked him.

"I kept getting more and more involved, and in December 1997, the Sunday before Christmas, we had a big dinner after the service. I was helping to tidy up, putting the chairs away, and suddenly it hit me just who Jesus was and why I needed him. I realized how broken I was and I went over to Chaplain Al, put my head on his shoulder, and cried and cried."

The people in the group smiled encouragingly. Several had already discovered who Jesus was and had made him central in their lives. But wherever people were in their own spiritual journeys, they resonated with the catharsis that Frank described. They knew what it was to weep and find release from the sadness and stress that had been so much a part of their lives.

Frank picked up his story. "I had been going to the college-and-career group, and one night in January 1998, it was at the pastor's house. I walked into the living room and the only seat left was beside a girl I hadn't noticed before. I sat down beside her, introduced myself, and started a conversation. I learned that her name was Tammy and that she was about fifteen years younger than me. We chatted for a while, though nothing was said that was particularly memorable to me, and before long I got up and mingled with the others.

"Time passed and at the next year's college-and-career Christmas party, I brought my partner, Matthew, and introduced him to Tammy. That's when she found out I was gay. She didn't seem too upset, and I learned later that she had several gay friends during high school. But I also learned later that she *was* upset, because at our very first meeting, the idea popped into her head that one day she would marry me."

Frank sat back, offering the floor to the next person in the circle. Before he could begin, cries of "what happened?" filled the room. Frank smiled. "It's a long story," he said. "I'll tell you more another time."

As the group leader, I knew attendance would be good at the next meeting. We were all hooked but, to be fair, others needed a chance to share.

31

Tito

One of the thoughts that kept recurring as I became integrated into the Christian community concerned how public I should go with my story. I began by telling my story to the church elders and then a few trusted friends. So far everything had gone well. Responses were generally positive, neutral at worst. I speculated that, for some, their acceptance of me may have been at least partly based on the fact that they didn't know what else to do. Yet I sensed I couldn't expect this to continue indefinitely.

On one occasion there was a small break in confidence, and I suddenly experienced some reserve, but even so, never a general backlash. Some family members of people who were informed without my consent stepped back somewhat from our relationship, though it was never broken. It seemed, though, that word didn't spread throughout the fellowship.

I couldn't help wondering if people would feel deceived somehow if I didn't make my story known to everyone, at least to some degree. The peer advice I received was mixed, and I really didn't know the right thing to do. I finally made my decision based on the advice of Dr. S. Lewis Johnson, professor at Dallas Theological Seminary. He was speaking at a conference in Toronto, and I contacted him where he was staying and asked if I could have a half hour of his time to discuss a serious personal decision I was facing.

He graciously agreed, and when we met, I didn't waste time in coming to the point. I briefly narrated my story and told him about my dilemma, laying out what I thought to be the best arguments for each course of action. I don't know if he had ever dealt with this kind of a situation before, but he was very kind. He reminded me that I was in the process of making a major life change in moving from gay to straight life. He noted that I would be facing some significant challenges in that alone. While he was very encouraging, he acknowledged the possibility of setbacks.

Given the circumstances, he believed it would not be helpful to add more potential roadblocks to my path. Rejection and even negativity would only discourage me and add to the challenges I was already facing. Taking everything into consideration, he advised me to stay on the course I had already adopted, informing people as I felt safe with them and on a need-to-know basis. This would ensure me the maximum amount of support while minimizing possible negative repercussions from people who didn't understand what God was doing in my life.

"Later, if there is a reason for more people to know, tell them as a testimony to the power of God in your life. But until that time comes, go slowly. Establish yourself firmly in the faith first." I found his counsel so wise and compassionate that I embraced it immediately. Over the years, I have shared my story with more and more people. Not all responses were as supportive as those crucial early ones were, but by then my confidence in God and my knowledge of myself had grown to the point where the negative ones didn't set me back. I have always been grateful for Dr. Johnson's input.

As I aligned my life more with God's purposes, I found the character of my relationships changing. I particularly developed a fondness for the seniors, and they reciprocated with enthusiasm. They opened their hearts and their homes to me, and I came to enjoy their company. They were appreciative of anything I was able to do for them, even if it was just to give them a bit of attention. One lady in particular informally "adopted" me. I often sat with her during services and accepted her frequent invitations to join her for Sunday dinner. Mrs. Kimmoff became a truly good friend as we shared a lot of time and our lives together. Her twin abilities as a cook and a conversationalist kept me coming back week after week.

For a time, a small group of the oldest members in the fellowship would get together about once a month in the home of one of them on a Sunday night after a service. For some reason, they always invited me. I felt honored to be included in this exclusive little group and, quite frankly, was never sure why they included me. I experienced a closeness with these older fellows and their wives that more than made up for my not having family nearby.

Between what I was learning in the support group and my firsthand experiences with my new Christian friends, I progressed to being comfortable in relationships with both men and women. For the first time in a long time, hugs, pats, and a hand on an arm or shoulder ceased to be loaded with sexual significance. They were merely expressions of affection, support, and care. As the old things passed away, everything became new.

My integration into the spiritual life at Greenwood continued over the years, to the point where I became involved more formally, particularly in working with the youth, in leading singing, and in opening services. These were the kinds of things that all of my peers in this local church were engaged in, and doing them made me feel "normal" and a real part of the group.

Christian fellowship played a crucial role for me in a couple of ways. First, it contributed significantly to my spiritual development as I learned by observing others while I also developed my own style of relating within the group. That they allowed me to cultivate my own identity among them mattered a lot to me as I didn't want to have to become someone else in order to be accepted. Second, though they may not always have known it, they became my lifeline in times of struggle.

Getting together with my Christian friends always refocused my attention from the struggle of the moment to something that lifted me up
rather than pulled me down.

My ongoing prayer times with Clara and Anna proved to be one of
the more helpful things in this regard, and it proved to be spiritually
fruitful not just to me but also in the lives of people with whom they
put me in touch. I had noticed that they sometimes prayed for a fellow
named Tito. I had met him but did not know him well. In his sixties,
Tito was not a regular part of the chapel and didn't fit in particularly
well. He seemed to have a talent for talking a lot, especially about whatever his burning issue was at the moment. Most often it had to do with
alternative medical treatments or the failings of current medical practice. He fidgeted almost constantly and often gave people the impression he was staring at them.

In response to a suggestion from Clara, I got in touch with him.
Since neither Tito nor I had a wife, children, or siblings nearby, Clara
thought he might be the kind of person with whom I could profit-
ably spend some time. The next time I saw him, I proposed getting
together for coffee. He agreed to the get-together part but said he'd prefer to drink something nonpoisonous and that the best place to do that
would be at his place because he could be sure that everything there was
healthy. Though his attitude put me off a bit, I agreed.

I made my way to his address and soon learned that Tito lived in a
building set aside by the city for subsidized housing in the gay village.
I called him on the intercom and he buzzed me in. He greeted me at
the door of his bachelor apartment and welcomed me into a small, tidy
space furnished only with a small table, two chairs, and a thin mattress
on the floor. What demanded my attention was the art that virtually
covered the walls. Tito loved European art from the seventeenth and
eighteenth centuries and had filled his tiny world with oversized views
of pastoral scenes, portraits, and religious themes popular in the era.

He served me herbal tea at the little table with tasteful candle accents
and as we chatted it became clear that he too had come out of the gay

lifestyle. That he still lived in the gay village didn't seem to be a problem for him, and though we stayed friends until his death several years later, we never discussed his old life. I never asked him about it and he never volunteered anything, though we both knew we shared a similar place in the present.

I learned that Tito had an Italian background and came from a staunch Catholic family. By the time I met him, his only relatives outside of Italy were his sister and her daughter. These two had little to do with him. His homosexuality and his later becoming a Protestant were more than enough cause for them to break ties with him. Mostly I felt pity for him because I couldn't honestly say he was a sympathetic character.

At first I wondered if he had AIDS. He was thin to the point of being skinny and had already lost all of his hair. His eyes were bulgy and his hands sometimes trembled. He did not look healthy. One thing that surprised me was how cool he kept his place. Guys with AIDS were usually cold; Tito seemed to be perpetually hot. He was certainly one of a kind, and with his problems and quirks, the guy needed a friend.

Tito was one of those people who have the misfortune of being the worst possible advertisement for their favorite cures. Considering his general sickliness, his appearance, and his lack of social skills, he would have been far more successful at convincing people to not take the concoctions of vitamins, minerals, and enzymes that he downed by the handful and made great claims for.

I knew I'd have to make a decision about Tito, so I consciously and deliberately chose to be his friend. I let his long health lectures roll off me and tried to divert his attention to spiritual things as quickly as possible. Tito truly loved the Lord and was happy to talk about him when I could get him on track. So over time, we became good friends, to the point that he considered me as a brother and even gave me a couple of pieces of his beloved art. He never hesitated to call me when he was in any kind of distress.

One day on my way to his place, it struck me that my relationship with Tito was unlike any other I had ever had. Here was a man I didn't really admire in any way, but at the same time, I had discovered a deep affection and care for him. I was shocked to think that God had used him to pull me out of my narcissism. After that I saw Tito as an instrument in God's hands—one which was slowly cutting away some of my own weaknesses even as he was building up positive qualities in me.

Forever restless, Tito eventually decided to join a Pentecostal church, where he felt more at home for a variety of reasons. Even though we no longer saw each other regularly at meetings, our friendship continued unabated, and his dependence on me grew. Sometimes when he was suffering from heart palpitations and insomnia, I would encourage him to go to a doctor. I even offered to take him, but he always refused. He was convinced that the medical system was a fraud and that God had put all we need for health in the vitamins and minerals which abounded in nature.

Tito was truly worthy of the title "gourmet cook." His kitchen boasted many cookbooks, especially ones featuring wholesome, organic ingredients. He cooked a lot with beans, grains, and seasonal vegetables. He made flatbread with tarragon flakes, which he served with olive oil, and fabulous salads with all kinds of exotic ingredients. Because of his ethnic heritage, he prepared a lot of Italian dishes. One of my favorites was stuffed zucchini loaded with minced peppers, tomatoes, mushrooms, ground beef, mozzarella cheese, and fresh herbs. He often cooked at my place because I had more space and was entirely happy to let him work away in the kitchen as I wrapped up my workday in the sign business.

One evening, as I was closing up shop and looking forward to a quiet evening at home alone watching a Blue Jays game, the phone rang. I wasn't really interested in doing more business that day, but I wasn't in a position to give my competitors the advantage simply because I couldn't be bothered to answer my phone.

"Sign In Please, Bob speaking," I said, as enthusiastically as I could.

There was a long silence on the other end of the line. All I could hear was the sound of someone trying to catch his breath.

"Hello, this is Bob at Sign In Please," I repeated. "Can I help you?"

"Bob," the voice in the receiver rasped, "help me."

"Tito," I asked, "is that you?"

"Yes." There was a long pause. "Can you come over? I need help."

"OK, buddy, I'll be there in ten minutes."

I quickly locked up, jumped into my car, and headed to Tito's place, wondering what kind of emergency I was about to get myself into.

Fortunately I was able to follow another resident in and went straight up the elevator to Tito's apartment. I knocked and tried the doorknob at the same time. It turned freely and I pushed the door open. There on the floor lay Tito, his limp fingers draped over the phone receiver near his head. His shirt was off and sweat glistened on his back. I knelt beside him.

"Tito, what happened? What's the matter?"

"Don't know," he slurred. "Help me up."

I had barely rolled him over and started to lift his torso when he signaled me to let him back down. He was gasping for breath. I put my ear to his chest and heard his rapid heartbeat.

"I'm calling an ambulance," I told him.

"Nooooo," he wailed weakly. "They'll kill me." He paused to catch his breath again. "Just help me up."

"Too late, buddy." I scooped the receiver off the floor and dialed 911.

I almost lost my friend that night. The ambulance came and took him off to the hospital. By then he was too weak to fight. I followed in my car, but they told me to go home and check in later. There was nothing I could do, and they had no time for me.

The next day I learned that they had diagnosed him with hyperthyroidism and had started treatments to regulate the unruly gland. Over the course of the next couple of weeks, they got his condition under control. Unfortunately, they didn't get Tito under control. In spite of all of the evidence pointing to a correct diagnosis and appropriate treatment, Tito never allowed himself to be convinced that the medical system had anything good about it.

When the time came to release him, he was still too sick to live alone, so I agreed to take him in. He stayed with me for the better part of a month. While he was with me, I persuaded him to take his medication. He acquiesced because he didn't have other viable living arrangements while he recuperated.

As soon as he went back home, he quickly reverted to his old pattern of living. We continued our friendship and he called me frequently to chat and to ask me to help around his place. He was one of those people who lives from crisis to crisis. On at least one other occasion, he ended up in the hospital for a couple weeks while doctors labored to bring him back from the brink of death. Though he was rescued several times by the health-care system, he never trusted it.

Our friendship lasted until he died of complications from his thyroid problem. Though he was a huge drain on my time and energy, I was sorry to see him go. He could have had many more years, but his choices cheated him out of them. For all he took from me and, on the surface, never gave back, I know God used him in my life to help me in my quests to draw closer to God and become more like Jesus.

32

Set Apart

From Frank's first time in the support group, he lived up to his name; he didn't hesitate to talk about his experiences, ideas, and challenges. For a leader, having someone like that in a group is a godsend. Sensing that I would look to Frank to keep discussions going in the lean times, I wanted to know more about him.

He and I began meeting occasionally for coffee in order to become better acquainted. I learned that Frank had a deep appreciation for the body of Christ in general and his own church fellowship in particular. After he became a believer, he found out that all the people at the church in Toronto were praying for him. Even members of the mother church in Pennsylvania were recruited to pray for him because they had a particular interest in reaching out to the gay community.

Not only did these two churches keep Frank before the Lord, but they were careful never to use condemning language, even as they made it clear that homosexual behavior did not fall within God's plan for human sexuality. Frank and other gay men in the group would frequently ask a pastor, "Is my being gay a sin?" This was a question that dogged us in our ministry to the LGBT community, so when Frank brought it up in one of our conversations, I was quick to ask him what his pastor said.

Frank smiled broadly and told me, "He'd say, 'Listen, Frank, you're asking the wrong question. What you really need to ask is, "Who is Jesus and what does it matter?" Because once you figure that out, the answer to all of your questions will be resolved.' And he was right. Usually, when one of us would ask that question, we'd be trying to pick a fight—trying to get him to say something condemning to serve our need for a stereotype to bash. But his response derailed the unproductive debate and pointed people to Jesus Christ in a way that he wouldn't have been able to if he'd answered the question in the way we expected him to right off the bat."

The more Frank told me about his pastor and the other people at their church, the more I admired them all. They had the right emphasis. People struggling with sin of all kinds need to stop focusing on it and look at the Lord Jesus Christ. Too many churches put more emphasis on getting a person to confess his or her sin than they do on helping that person to know Jesus Christ, who he is, and what he's all about. I liked the way Frank could speak with authority about the fact that it is the Holy Spirit who transforms lives. We can't clean ourselves up, so insisting that people do that before they can experience salvation is a nonstarter.

However, I still was curious about the purity issue. It was lovely that the people in this church didn't communicate condemnation as they reached out to Frank, but my own understanding of the Bible generated some tension in me over this approach, and I asked Frank the inevitable follow-up question, "So didn't anyone challenge you about the sin in your life?"

"Of course," Frank said. "The church can never condone sin of any kind. But here's the deal: until a person has accepted Jesus and has the Holy Spirit's power in his or her life, meaningful, lasting change is impossible. Secular gays are right when they say, 'I can't change.' They really can't. But once a gay person has accepted Jesus, and the Holy Spirit is present, he can be challenged about what he's going to do with his sexuality.

"Again though, Bob," he continued, "this calls for wisdom. When people challenged me about my behavior, I still tended to get defensive. That always had the effect of hardening my position. What disarmed me most effectively was when people challenged me about my beliefs. My pastor, in particular, kept pressing me to make my beliefs line up with what I was reading in the Bible. His pushing challenged me to look at myself in light of Christ. That was what the Holy Spirit used in my life to do his work of transforming me."

One of the things that Frank and I talked about was the issue of identity. He told me about friends who dared to question whether he really was who he thought he was. No one, gay or straight, enjoys this kind of confrontation, and Frank confessed to being extremely angry with people who did this—mostly because it associated an element of choice with being gay. This is the one thing gays don't want to consider. After all, if there is any choosing at all, then it could be argued that we should be making other choices, and for most active gays that is unthinkable.

"So how did you deal with the issue?" I asked him. "I know the process I had to go through to know myself. What about you?"

Frank paused thoughtfully before responding. "Gradually, I read and thought more about these issues and discovered that what I had always thought had gaps in it. I learned that the development of same-sex attraction can start as early as conception, based on the emotional environment of the home. Factors like the child being unwanted, or not being of the preferred sex, can have an impact. I can only remember back as far as age four, but I know I had done a lot of developing as a person before then. I felt I had to honestly consider these ideas, and the more I did, the more I accepted the possibility that I had made mistakes as I tried to develop an understanding of why I was the way I was.

"Weeks of inner turmoil went by, but I got to the point where I could finally admit to myself that I wasn't who I had always told myself I was. When I did that, I suddenly felt about four inches taller. I felt so much relief. You might think I would have felt loss because of the identity I was walking away from, but I didn't. I really sensed that I had been living a lie."

"Now, there's a strong word," I said.

"But sometimes you have to call a lie what it is." He raised his voice a little for emphasis. "Remember, I wasn't your average gay guy; I was politically gay as well. The political position I had espoused told me that until I came out as gay in high school, I had been living a lie. I heard and read this many times because the idea is heavily reinforced in the gay scene. I repeated this 'truth' many times myself, though looking back, I'm not sure if I was trying to convince other people or myself. Either way, under the influence of this idea, I accepted that I was gay and went through the process of coming out. At the time, I thought that when I came out of the closet, I had begun to live the 'truth.'

"Bob, you've been on the inside, you get this, but I sometimes ask my straight friends, 'Can you imagine living with this understanding for thirty-five years only to learn that this "truth" was really the biggest lie of all?' When I embraced the truth of my masculinity, I felt a burden lift."

I did know what he was talking about. I also knew what it cost me in terms of friendships with my gay friends, so I asked Frank about that.

"When I told Matthew, his response was, 'So you want to experiment with women? Go experiment. I'll give you a month!' I said, 'No, no, it's more than that. I don't just want a month. I'm getting out.' And I terminated the relationship."

Frank was amazingly open about both his sexuality and his spirituality. On one occasion, the discussion in the support group turned to spiritual crises, which many group members had been through. Before long, Frank joined the interaction with his account of a moment when everything had changed for him. He reminded us that he was already a believer—that is, he had accepted that Jesus died on the cross in his place to free him from the consequences of sin. But he had yet to learn that Jesus wanted to also set him free from sin itself, not just its consequences.

One day as we were chatting, I suddenly became aware that Frank had made very rapid progress, faster than anyone else I knew who was traveling the same road. I started probing around to see if there was anything in his past which might have prepared him spiritually to accept that God was there and interested in his life.

He told me that early in his adult life, as he cycled through relationships, he realized that something wasn't working for him, so he consulted a psychiatrist. When the doctor heard the outline of his life, he told him that he should consider himself to be a sex addict and seek treatment. This didn't surprise me a great deal. A lot of my gay friends had struggled with this sensation of "not being able to get enough." But as Frank looked into treatment for the addictive aspect of his personality and its expression through sex, he was brought face-to-face with something unexpected.

Frank told me, "All of my spirituality to this point was of the New Age variety, looking to 'the god within.' When I got involved in a twelve-step program for sex addicts, I was confronted with the idea of 'a higher power.' To this point in my life, I was the ultimate power. I felt no need to look outside myself for a frame of reference as to what was good, or normal, or natural. If I wanted to do it, it was natural. If it was natural, it was normal. If it was normal, it was good.

"Suddenly this program forced me to at least superficially accept the presence of a higher power in my life. I remember some guy telling me, 'Listen, Frank. There is a higher power and you're not it.' So it was this program that began to open my mind to the reality of God— something I'd never honestly considered before. That was very helpful and set the stage for things that would come later. Things like meeting Chaplain Al, then Pastor Stephen, and others God would use to keep leading me along the path I was on."

At one of our support-group meetings, Frank described how a University of Toronto Christian campus group invited his own pastor as one of their keynote speakers for some public sessions in one of the lecture theaters. Pastor Stephen, in turn, invited any interested members of his church to attend his session. Frank went along with a few others.

"At the end of the session," Frank told us, "Pastor Stephen gave an altar call, inviting anyone who wanted to publicly confess Jesus as his Savior to join him at the front of the theater. Though I had been calm to that point, a struggle arose in me. I thought, *You know what, Frank? You need to do this now or walk away from this whole Christian thing and never go back.* After a moment of indecision, I stood up and went forward. That was a turning point for me. That was when true repentance happened. I thought, *Enough is enough. This all has to stop.* And I stopped all of my sexual acting out, cold turkey."

At that, some in the group applauded. We knew it was true because Frank was so . . . well, frank. If he told us that was what had happened, that was exactly what had happened. No one doubted Frank's word. I encouraged him to tell us what happened after that.

"I needed to get a job to support myself because I gave up the massage business. I went to an air-conditioning trade show looking for a job and got one. That was one step. Another was getting out of the environment where everyone knew who I was and what I did. Soon I located an apartment in Etobicoke, far enough from the gay scene that I didn't have to deal with the constant parade of triggers for acting out sexually.

"I also lost my hostility toward the ideas that I had found so upsetting just a few weeks earlier. I read the books suggested by my friends and let myself accept their message of hope for a different kind of life. It was around this time Pastor Stephen suggested I look into ministries that were reaching out to guys in my situation. I checked out a few and ended up here."

Spontaneous applause broke out again. Many of the people in the group that day related strongly to Frank's story. It was an exhilarating session.

Not many weeks later, Frank confided in me that his relationship with Tammy was deepening. He disclosed that they had become emotionally intimate, sharing details of their lives with each other, encouraging and supporting each other, and sensing a deep bond. I asked him if he thought there was anything inappropriate about their relationship.

His only concern was that he was starting to feel that a relationship with that level of connection had to have some responsibility attached to it in order to protect it as well as Tammy and himself.

Over the course of the next few months, Tammy came into more and more conversations. Sometimes her name would be mentioned in comments to the whole group. I began to consider the possibility that their relationship might develop to the point of marriage. I wasn't sure just what to do with that. The ministry didn't have heterosexual marriage as the goal for all the gay men it helped; we were chiefly interested in pointing people to Christ.

Interacting with people in the support group was a highlight of my life. I enjoyed seeing them open up. The fragile ones became a little more resilient, the cocky ones a little more humble, the self-confident ones a little more dependent on the Holy Spirit. One of the big issues that is tied into being gay is identity. Most heterosexual people don't go around thinking of themselves as "opposite-sex attracted" several times a day. They just are. Many in the gay community are almost continuously aware that they are gay. This may be, at least in part, due to their being a minority, but speaking from my own experience, there's more to it than that.

Being gay sets us apart. It gives us an identity and a sense of superiority because we're different from the mainstream. Some people in this world are great artists. Some people are talented singers. Some are athletes. Some are entrepreneurial and can turn almost anything into money. All such labels serve as forms of identity. Similarly, being gay provides gay people with identity. One day I chatted with Frank about this and he agreed. "I didn't find identity in any of the things most others do, but I knew who I was as a sexual partner. I would always default to sexual behavior whenever I was insecure, lonely, even hungry, tired, or bored."

"What do you mean?" I asked.

"My sexual activities affirmed who I was as a person, including who I was sexually. Way back when, my male identity was rejected, though

I've never been able to identify a specific event that triggered it. It could easily have happened before I was old enough to have memories. Whatever may have initiated it, I spent years trying to get it back. The way I chose to do it was by cannibalizing the maleness of other men by having sex with them. For years, I didn't realize that the aspect of my identity that was missing was my role as a child of God. It was spiritual.

"Sexual union is probably as close as you can get to spiritual union, so that's how it is easily confused. It's also why becoming a follower of Jesus is so important. It restores the piece of the puzzle that is missing in every life. Once I accepted Jesus Christ as the one who had given himself for me, and once I received the Holy Spirit, I began to change. Rather, I should say, God began changing me—changing my identity from the inside out. I came to understand and accept that I am perfectly male because God created me that way. I don't have to have sex with men to become more masculine. The fact of my maleness was established at conception."

One of the life lessons I tried to communicate to my support-group members was the issue of healthy boundaries, particularly physical ones. Merely being casually physical in the gay scene can quickly erode social boundaries, paving the way for a sexual encounter.

This was a major hurdle in my own life, and I found it to be true generally among the men I worked with. Discovering that you can have close relationships with men, even ones that involve touching—like putting a comforting arm around a shoulder or squeezing an arm in encouragement—without ending up in a sexual encounter came as a shock to nearly all of us who had spent years in the gay scene.

In the support group, we worked toward helping the members identify the issues related to the expression of their sexuality. Over the years, hundreds of people went through the program, learning about how to be whole persons without abusing themselves or others in compulsive sexual activity.

After a year at the support-group level, those who were interested in going deeper with the spiritual aspect of things were invited to move on into the growth group I was facilitating, which included both group work and one-on-one mentoring. The growth group shifted attention from personal sexual issues to maturing in our relationship with God. Getting set on the right trajectory with God has a huge positive impact on human relationships, and some of the men we were working with started to think about dating and marriage by the time we were wrapping up the growth-group phase of the program.

About every six weeks or so, we'd have a social function to which the fellows could bring their girlfriends or wives. This gave us a chance to have low-pressure social relationships with both sexes. One of the first women to join us was Frank's friend Tammy. They were formally dating at the time, though their relationship was mostly still a friendship.

Their moment of insight finally came when Frank had an opportunity to go to China. They both realized they couldn't live without each other. Frank proposed. Tammy accepted without batting an eye, and the stage was set for their coming together as husband and wife.

However, there were obstacles. As well as they knew each other, their lives couldn't have been much more different. Their age difference and their having lived in different cultures for most of their lives were bound to present some challenges, so they undertook premarital counseling to sort out some of the unavoidable issues. They also leaned heavily on their friends during this time. They lived. They learned. They struggled. They cried. But eventually the big day rolled around. We all pitched in, and a new, though somewhat unlikely, couple was united in the bonds of holy matrimony.

33

Bert

My own development, both personally and spiritually, continued to progress. The more time I spent with my new friends at church, the more I experienced their warmth and compassion. They often prayed for people who found themselves in adverse circumstances: relationship problems, employment needs, health concerns. However, they didn't limit themselves to prayer. They sent cards and flowers, prepared and delivered meals, and visited the sick and lonely. I enjoyed the shift into active ministry as I became more integrated into the life of the fellowship. My extroverted personality allowed me to feel comfortable reaching out to others even if I didn't personally know them.

Clara told me about Bert when he was in the hospital for a hip replacement and in need of some company. The next time I had an hour available, I dropped in at the orthopedic hospital to see him. Bert was in his mid fifties, relatively short with a medium build. Though he'd spent some days confined to bed because of hip-replacement surgery, he was nevertheless carefully groomed, his white hair neatly combed, with no sign of bedhead. Outgoing by nature, he welcomed me instantly, though we had barely met before, and introduced me to another visitor. Within seconds, I recognized that Bert and his friend were both gay. From the way they interacted, it seemed that Bert's visitor was an old boyfriend. I stayed just long enough to introduce myself, mention a few friends we had in common at the chapel, and promise to come back again sometime.

The next time I visited Bert he was alone, and we had a chance to become acquainted. I told him I was just another single guy, recently connected to the chapel and looking for some friends for mutual encouragement. He seemed pleased by my gesture of friendship and plunged into a description of his plans for the gardens around the chapel come spring. His enthusiasm for the beauty of nature and his creativity expressed through gardening were insuppressible.

Before I left that day, Bert told me he was healing well after his surgery and he looked forward to being released within the next couple of days. I told him I'd visit him at home and was pleased to learn that he lived near me, between my place on Broadview and the chapel. He told me he'd call me as soon as he was settled at home and ready for a visit.

Peter at the gay ministry had encouraged me to develop healthy, nonsexual friendships with both men and women, and I hoped Bert would be someone with whom I could do that. Knowing he had been active as a homosexual assured me he'd know where I was coming from and would be able to understand me in ways my new straight friends couldn't. True to his word, Bert called and asked me to come to his home the next evening at seven o'clock for a visit and to help him with a couple of small chores.

When I arrived at his home, he complimented me on my punctuality and led me into his kitchen. He had retired from his work as a justice of the peace and had carefully stewarded his resources so that his surroundings could reflect his taste for fine things. His house looked as if it had been prepared for a magazine photo shoot—not extravagant but spotlessly clean, with everything meticulously arranged for the best effect. He gestured to a chair for me; then, gripping his walker, he took his place in the matching one facing me at a slight angle across the corner of the kitchen table. I noticed that his customary seat provided a splendid view of his picturesque back garden. A small telephone table within easy reach held a selection of gardening magazines interspersed with some religious publications.

Bert grimaced slightly as his weight settled into the chair.

"Still hurt a bit?" I asked.

"Yes," he replied, his dignified British accent adding a crispness to the word. "I'm still somewhat uncomfortable, but I learned from my previous experience that the best thing is to keep as active as I can. It hurts to move, but if I stay immobile for too long, the discomfort escalates to the point of outright pain."

"How long have you been in Canada?" I asked.

"I came over about thirty years ago."

"By yourself?"

"Yes," he replied. "No one else in the family was prepared to make the move. They've visited me a few times, and I go back home to see them as opportunities arise. But I can't say I'm homesick. I'm quite settled here now and am content to spend the rest of my days in Canada."

Eventually our conversation shifted to gardening. Horticulture was something in which he had developed an interest while still a boy in England. During his early days in Toronto, Bert had taken to recreating the gardens he had enjoyed back home. This provided a link for him and gave him an outlet for his creative energy. It also provided for some modest notoriety as he won prizes for the best residential garden in East York.

As twilight faded into darkness, I reminded Bert that he had something he wanted me to do for him.

"Ah, yes. I've found our conversation so satisfying that I'd forgotten about that. It will soon be time for me to begin preparing the flower beds around the house, and I thought perhaps you'd be willing to bring my gardening things out of the basement where they've been stored for the winter. They aren't particularly heavy, but I find it awkward handling them on the stairs and manipulating them through doors in my debilitated state."

He pulled himself to his feet and led me to the basement stairway at the side of the house. An outside door opened onto a landing, three steps down. He flipped on the light switch at the top of the stairs before heading down. He navigated the stairs better than I expected but had to hang on to the railings on both sides. I could see why he needed help to carry anything, especially long-handled gardening tools.

The basement was typical of old Toronto homes of the time: dim and a little damp, with a characteristic fragrance supplied by old coal dust embedded in the floor joists overhead and the unpainted concrete floor underfoot. But that's where the comparison stopped. Everything was as clean as it could be and neatly arranged. The garden tools, which had been washed before being stored and misted with oil to keep them from rusting, were hung from a couple of racks made from two-by-fours with four-inch spikes driven into them at precise locations. A hose was neatly coiled on a reel, which was set in a small, green, two-wheeled garden cart. Trowels, a bulb planter with the depths clearly marked in inches, and a three-pronged hand cultivator were also in the cart.

"If you don't mind, I'd appreciate your taking all of these things up the stairs and out the side door," Bert said. "I have a place at the back of the house for them during the gardening season, but I don't like to leave them out over the winter."

We returned up the stairs but exited at the side door. He showed me where he wanted his things put and then opened and closed the door for me as I made half a dozen trips with my arms full of tools. When we were finished, we returned inside.

Back in the kitchen, Bert made us a pot of tea and took some purchased biscuits from the cupboard, arranging them on a plate while apologizing for not having been able to bake any himself. "Of all the things I missed while in the hospital, working in my kitchen was the most distressing. I love to bake and cook." He paused to close the package and return it to its place. "One day, I'll cook for you, Bob. You'll have to tell me what you like."

"I haven't discovered anything that I don't like. That should keep it simple for you."

He smiled. "I'll take you at your word."

As we had our tea and biscuits, Bert shifted the conversation from gardening to cooking and told tales of meals ranging from triumphs (mostly his) to disasters (mostly other people's). I was thoroughly charmed by the man. I appreciated his neatness, though he went several notches beyond what I considered my own rather high standard, and I enjoyed his conversational skills as well. Our connection was mutual and comfortable, and I expected that Bert and I would become good friends.

Both Tito and Bert had given up their gay ways, but our relationships were very dissimilar. Tito taught me to sacrifice. He was so demanding that I found myself constantly reordering my personal priorities so I could respond to him with generosity of spirit. With Tito I was constantly on guard against our relationship degenerating into codependency.

Everything was different with Bert. He taught me the importance of balance, and we developed a healthy relationship with give and take.

That spring Bert needed quite a bit of help with his gardening and I found myself at the top of his on-call list. However, I hardly ever helped him without his serving up a wonderful meal. These were usually drawn from his love of classic English fare. His favorites soon became mine as I enjoyed the personal touch he added to roast beef with Yorkshire pudding, or fish and chips featuring his own batter recipe (which he never saw fit to share with me). Sometimes, he'd send me home with fresh-baked bread or some other delight he'd just pulled from his oven.

Just as the practical areas of our relationship were balanced, so was our conversation. We both liked to talk, but we both listened as well. While we didn't pretend that our gay years didn't exist, we didn't discuss that aspect of our lives in depth. I think both of us wanted to preserve what we had in our friendship and didn't want to risk it by talking about things that might trigger responses we were both anxious to leave behind.

As we spent more time together and enjoyed our high level of compatibility, we quickly learned that we had a few differences. I had correctly identified Bert's former boyfriend when I first met them both during Bert's hospitalization. As far as Bert was concerned, the sexual aspect of his relationship with Richard was forever behind them, and he had no qualms about continuing the friendship. In fact, Richard and I enjoyed roughly the same status in Bert's life, and they remained buddies until Bert's death.

I challenged Bert about this, because being alone with an old boyfriend would make it difficult for me to keep my thoughts where I wanted them to be. Maybe I had a better memory than he did, but seeing one of my former partners could unleash a flood of memories that I preferred to avoid. Bert didn't seem to struggle with this. He insisted that since he had decided to put homosexuality behind him, he not only could but *should* continue to spend time with Richard. "How else could I show him the new freedom I have?" he would ask.

Not having a good answer for that question helped me to see that we all have our own course through life, each with his own areas of temptation and triumph.

Bert did all the gardening around the chapel as well as kept his own property looking like a proper English garden. The more time we spent together, the better I became acquainted with him and the things that made him special. He loved his little bungalow, which benefited from what amounted to an obsession with cleanliness. Every week Bert washed his windows inside and out. He had beautiful things and kept everything spotless and perfect. Eventually I learned that much of his furniture had been custom made for him. I say "eventually" because, even though we were friends, I knew him for more than a year before he invited me into the living room.

His car was as clean as his house. Besides washing it at least once a week, he'd have it professionally detailed every month or so to keep it perpetually looking new. He was organized, but managed to work some flexibility into his schedule to make room for an active social life. His kindness and generosity spilled over to bless all who knew him.

As years passed, our friendship deepened. We learned a lot from each other because we became so close, but that closeness gave rise to some

sharp disagreements. We were both adult men who had lived inde-
pendently for more than twenty years. We had our own ways of doing
things and many deeply held views on everything from housekeeping
to theology. It would have been easy to walk away when we argued, but
because of the superficiality of our relationships in the past, we valued
what we had. Rather than letting our differences divide us, we chose to
let them deepen our respect for each other.

One of the things we hammered out between us was a consistent
view of the role of accountability in our relationship. Accountability
certainly has a place as Christian friends hold each other responsible to
maintain a godly standard in their attitudes and behavior. Yet it also has
a downside because sessions of probing questions and honest answers
can keep the focus on the problem rather than on the Lord. We learned
that drawing each other's attention to Christ as the model for our lives
was much more helpful than constantly challenging each other about
our confessed weaknesses.

Our mutual care helped us both grow. I was particularly gratified
to see how the Lord used me to build into the life of another believer.
During the years we shared as friends, I saw Bert grow in his love for the
Lord and his relationships with the people at Greenwood. He became
increasingly active in church, sometimes opening a service, sharing a
devotional thought from the Bible, or leading in prayer.

Bert's contribution to my life was to help me develop spiritual fruit in
areas like patience, forbearance, and peace. He was ridiculously punc-
tual and typically demanding in that regard. At first I reacted nega-
tively, but soon I learned that he was not going to change, and if our
friendship was to thrive, I'd have to adjust to his view of time. Looking
back, it was a small sacrifice, but it softened my heart to the idea of
adjusting my own, often strongly held views for the sake of my brothers
and sisters.

When Bert was sixty, his health began to fail significantly. Besides
having undergone three hip-replacement surgeries, he'd had numerous
gastrointestinal problems over the years which came to a crisis rather

suddenly. Nothing could be done for him medically but to keep him as comfortable as possible. I spent even more time with him in his last days than had been my custom before. It was a comfort for me to know that he was never lonely in his final decline.

After the funeral, Richard, who served as his executor, contacted me to tell me that Bert had specifically designated a number of his prized possessions to come to me. To this day, I have several keepsakes and pieces of furniture in my home which I treasure because they remind me of Bert and our friendship.

34

The Uphill Road

had been so busy with my own life that I didn't notice Frank and Tammy drifting out of it. Shortly after their wedding, the growth-group cycle came to an end, so we weren't brought together by the program any longer, and since we lived in different parts of the city, our paths didn't cross much. We lost track of each other.

The better part of three years had gone by when, out of the blue, the phone rang one Saturday evening. It was Frank. After going through the obligatory catching up that friends do after they've been separated too long, he got to the reason for the call.

"Bob, it's been great reconnecting, but I actually have a specific reason for calling," he said. "Tammy asked me to get in touch with you again, because"—he paused briefly—"things haven't been going so well for me."

"Oh! Tell me about that."

"To give you the short version, I just got back from a business trip in the States. I met a guy on the plane and . . . well, I made a bad judgment call. Right away I felt terrible for betraying Tammy. I knew I'd made a wrong choice, and I knew I'd have to tell Tammy about it. When I got home, I did that. She was hurt and upset, of course. I tried to say the right things, but nothing I expressed seemed to fall into that category.

Finally she told me she thought I should call you. Given that we weren't making much progress on our own, it seemed like my best option. So here I am."

"Well, Frank, I clearly don't have to tell you that you've blown it. Tell me how you're doing spiritually."

It was so quiet that for a moment I thought the call had been dropped. Then he said, "To tell the truth, Bob, nothing much is happening in that department."

"I assume that means you're not reading your Bible much, or praying, or spending time with other Christians."

"That's a fair assumption. I'm not really doing any of those things at all."

Feeling hurt and disappointed, I blurted, "You're spiritually bankrupt, Frank. How can you think of living in this world—in this battle—when your soul is empty? You've drained your spiritual bank account and aren't doing anything to fill it."

Another long silence showed he had nothing to say.

"Frank, you need to get back into the zone where you were when you were in the growth group. You were tracking well then. You were honoring God and building your relationship with Tammy. How was that going before this recent disaster?"

"Not great. She's been busy since the baby came along. We've been drifting apart a bit."

I shook my head, though I knew he couldn't see. "Listen, man, you've got to get serious. You need to be praying, drawing on God's strength for you, every day. Stay fresh and keep clean. Like you do with your physical body, Frank. Sometimes a quick shower will be enough; other times you need a long, luxurious bath in the Word of God to get you clean. Either way, you need to practice some spiritual hygiene. When you don't, Frank, you start to stink."

Obviously, the Holy Spirit was already at work in him or he wouldn't have been able to receive all that, especially the last bit. Before we hung up, I also encouraged him to get back to church with Tammy and asked him to keep in touch. That was the beginning of the reestablishment of our relationship. One of us would call the other every couple of weeks or so, and we made a point of getting together occasionally. Over the following months, I could see the spiritual spark coming back into his life.

A few years ago I bought a farm, and Frank and Tammy became part of the circle of friends who visit me there sometimes to help with chores, or play with the horses, or just sit by the woodstove, sipping tea and chatting. They particularly like to bring their children, Ben and Molly, to expose them to country life and acquaint them with "Uncle Bob." From the first time I laid eyes on them, I felt like they were grandchildren to me.

On one visit, while the kids were out playing with the dogs, the conversation turned to Frank's spiritual turnaround.

"Bob," said Frank, "it was shortly after that awkward phone call that our family relationship began to flourish again. I started enjoying being a husband to my wife and a father to my son, and now a dad to little Molly. But that slip on my part damaged our marriage, and Tammy would frequently ask me if I was OK."

"Especially when Frank was traveling," Tammy jumped in. "As he was preparing to go, I'd look him in the eye and ask, 'Are you in a safe place?' I'd wait for him to affirm that he was before I'd let him go."

"But I needed it," he said. "It was part of what made things right. I wasn't going to hurt her again. And your advice has paid off, along with Tammy's love and understanding. I've developed new ways of thinking and new patterns of behavior. There are places I can safely go today where if I'd gone ten years ago, I'm pretty sure I would have fallen. So there is victory. But there is vulnerability as well. All the victory in the world doesn't completely remove the vulnerability."

"That's a lesson you can't learn too soon," I said.

"It's kinda funny." Frank smiled. "I used to just struggle with same-sex attractions; now I struggle with opposite-sex attractions too. I struggle with a lot of things."

"At least you're struggling," I said. "It's when you give up the fight that you're beat. Do you tell Tammy about your struggles? Are you two able to share them?"

Tammy nodded as Frank said, "I sometimes hate to tell her, but openness has been the key for me. As soon as I'd get into my secret space, I could sense Satan getting a foothold in my life to tempt me."

"Secrecy splits relationships," Tammy chimed in.

"For a while I thought I had it all under control," Frank said. "I learned that it was foolish for me to think I was impervious to temptation. Even though I'm much stronger now than I was, I'm aware that tracks were laid down in my mind for the first almost forty years of my life, and they will take me in the wrong direction if I'm not conscious and intentional about where I choose to go and what I choose to do. I've had to undo my patterns of thinking, and that has taken much longer and been much more challenging than I ever imagined."

I kept pushing, because I wanted to assure myself that things were as good as they seemed. "Are you able to be open with others as well as Tammy?" I asked. "I mean Christian peers and leaders."

"I've learned to dismantle the barriers," he said. "Old habits die hard, and one of the things I did when I was living in the gay scene was shut out people from the straight community, creating barriers, and then blame them for not being there for me. I try not to do that anymore, and when I see the old pattern repeating itself, I do something intentional to stop it.

"When people refused to argue with me, I was disarmed. I had nothing to push against when I was surrounded by people who reached out to me. I never sensed judgment or condemnation from them related to my engaging in homosexual practices. Instead they said things like, 'Hey, can you come to my house for a meal?' or 'Can I help you move?' or 'Would you like to go to a concert?' They were loving me in a way I could recognize."

I jumped in. "But, Frank, you have to admit that it took awhile. You were a long time coming, as I recall."

"That's fair. It didn't happen quickly. I was a pretty militant gay. I liked to talk with moneyed and political types and lay down the law to them about how society was going to have to adjust for me and others like me. So I confess that I was resistant. I was suspicious. It was the constant gestures of genuine love that made me start to dismantle the walls I had put up to them as people and to their views about sexuality. I have to say that no one I know has ever been successfully argued out of homosexuality."

"Absolutely not!" I shook my head, thinking about some of the misguided attempts on the part of Christians to convince my gay friends that they should leave the life. I had seen some guys badgered into saying they were straight when they weren't. Others would even accept all the arguments about risky behavior, promiscuity, and so on, but that didn't change their attitudes or behavior.

"You're right, Frank. I've never known anyone who was argued out of homosexuality, but I've seen them loved out."

"I was loved out," Frank agreed. "Loved out by people who put me ahead of their own preferences and tendencies. Loved out by people with near-infinite patience. Loved out by people who were in it for the long haul and never stopped loving me as weeks turned into months, which turned into years."

Tammy spoke up. "From what I've seen, arguing against someone is the best way to reinforce what they're doing. You have both seen guys who were confronted about their lives go back to their gay friends and say, 'It's true. Christians hate us. They don't accept us. They want us to change or they won't love us.' So the stereotype is strengthened and the gulf gets wider."

I said, "I don't know what it is, but somehow, being threatened with consequences doesn't make a bit of difference. I had all kinds of people tell me I should give up cigarettes too. They told me all about what was likely to happen to me statistically, and I'd blow smoke in their faces. Sometimes literally. When I quit, I did so for my own reasons, not anyone else's."

"I've learned about consequences," said Frank. "In the past, I mostly disregarded the consequences of my lifestyle. Looking back, I can only see God's hand of protection on me. I mean, I had thousands of sex partners and never got HIV/AIDS. I take no credit for that, because I acted out in unbelievably risky ways. Now that I'm married, have children, and am deeply involved in a local church, I'm aware that the consequences of my behavior will not just touch my own life. Other innocent people, many of whom trust me and look to me as an example, will be affected by the outcomes of any chances I take."

As we chatted, we confirmed that it doesn't matter what sin issue anyone struggles with, the one we were most familiar with or one we wouldn't consider; it is the body of Christ, the hands and feet of Jesus, that loves others into the family of God. Frank reminded us how Jesus dealt with people in his day—the woman at the well, the tax collectors, the prostitutes, and so on. He loved his enemies, those who lived in opposition to all he stood for.

Jesus let his social circle overlap with their social circle. He didn't just hang out with his disciples—his own inner circle. The church needs to learn from this. Few Christians have many (or any) friends who are not also Christians. Though they might work with some, and real friendships can develop in workplaces, it is rare. At work, you're thrown together and you have to function together for some other purpose. Friends are mutually chosen. Most Christians only choose other Christians as friends. This is understandable on one level, but taking Christ as our example, it falls short.

The church that loved Frank to Christ tried to follow a first-century model. They reached out to everyone, especially people who were being ignored or marginalized by other churches. One of the big differences between Jesus and his church today is that Jesus was prepared to walk with people who often stumbled on the road to spiritual maturity. Peter comes to mind as an example. The church today typically wants some kind of up-front assurance that you, as a sexual sinner of any kind, can demonstrate that you have not just been forgiven but miraculously, permanently set free from temptation. They want you to look them in the eye and declare, without even a hint of wavering, that you will never fall into sexual sin again. Of course, that's simply not possible.

They're not quite as demanding in the areas of other sins. They might be prepared to cut an alcoholic or a thief some slack, but people who slip into their old sexual sins from time to time tend to be quickly dismissed from the fellowship, either formally or informally. We kid ourselves if we think that sexual sin is "the big one" that must be completely and irrevocably abandoned to be worthy of fellowship. How many "good Christians" are angry people? Like sex addicts, they are simply following the tracks they've laid down over a lifetime of feeling grieved and offended when things don't go their way. Yet the Bible is clear that human anger doesn't produce righteousness (James 1:19–20).

As soon as we start looking at other people's sin as worse than our own, we've already fallen into the sin of pride. The Bible commands us not to think of ourselves more highly than we ought (Romans 12:3). And, of course, some people have both problems at the same time. Maybe most people have both problems at the same time. Lack of opportunity may keep them from acting out sexually, but there's nothing to hinder them from lording their perceived holiness over everyone else, even as they wallow in illicit desire.

Ben and Molly's return with the dogs shut down the conversation that day. But before leaving the discussion here, let me be clear that one person's sin does not justify another person's sin. Jesus told his disciples to both get rid of the plank in their own eye *and* remove the speck from their brother's eye once they themselves could see clearly (Matthew 7:1–5).

35

Elizabeth

Among the first people I met at Greenwood Gospel Chapel was a tall, gentle woman with a ready smile and a warm personality. We saw each other at meetings and social events but didn't really develop a friendship until the following summer in 1992, when a group of us went to Camp Galilee in the Ottawa Valley for a week. As we spent time together during that week, I came to appreciate her spiritual sensitivity and her gift of encouragement. I quickly learned that she loved to help and was always ready to assist anyone who needed anything, whether it was moving a piece of lawn furniture or completing a foursome for shuffleboard.

When we returned to Toronto we pursued a friendship. I liked her a great deal because she was down to earth, friendly, and caring—all characteristics I admired. I suppose it was inevitable that a lot of our friends assumed we had a romantic relationship, though it never was for me and was only briefly for her. It was only after we'd known each other for a couple of years that she told me she had spent a few weeks wondering if there was a deeper chemistry between us, but she decided it was best to keep our relationship at the friendship level. That's where it remains, and I believe time has proven that, for us, this has been best.

Soon after our return from camp, we started going places together.

Liz is spontaneous and brings a lot of light and laughter to any social interaction. At the time, several of us at Greenwood enjoyed the spontaneity available to single adults without family responsibilities. Sometimes we'd suddenly decide to pack a picnic lunch and go to Kew Beach or some such place, just for the pleasure of being with each other.

The house on Broadview, where I operated my sign-making business, was my focus around the time Liz and I met, and sometimes she and a couple of other friends would come over and help with pulling the house apart and putting it together again. She showed an amazing willingness to pitch in, and I appreciated all the help I could get in those days because I was trying to do things as inexpensively as possible.

Liz regularly included me in her social circle. She was very hospitable and would often invite me when she had other friends to her place. It was after one of these occasions that I decided to risk telling her my story. She listened compassionately and then confided that she wasn't surprised. I'm not sure what tipped her off, as I had always tried to avoid "gayisms" in my speech and behavior. I felt blessed that she never showed anything but acceptance either before or after I confirmed her suspicions that I had spent a large part of my life in the gay scene.

While we consciously decided long ago not to pursue a romance, I include Liz among my best friends. As happens in any long friendship, we've had times when we were less close, and we're both OK with that. We have many other good friends besides each other. We've both seen codependent relationships and have no desire to fall into that trap. We have some friends in common, but not all.

Fifty years ago, unmarried people were assumed not to be sexually active. These days, unmarried adults are assumed to be sexually active or religious fanatics or somehow defective. I confess it has been a challenge to live in this kind of environment. It requires more explaining than either of us enjoys, but it's the reality we live in. One of Satan's biggest lies is that you can't be a normal person without being sexually active. That assumption is false.

On October 27, 2011, Frank, Tammy, Ben, and Molly came to spend the day, and I invited Liz to join us for a day in the country. We were all enjoying the crisp fall weather, playing with the dogs and horses and puttering around doing odd jobs while the kids played. It occurred to me that some fresh apple crisp would be a great end to the evening meal, and I asked Liz if she'd mind picking a few apples from the big old trees in my front yard. Always agreeable, she nodded and went off to find a basket in the garage and then headed off to my mini orchard. I told her about the ladder—a kind of a three-legged stepladder designed specifically for orchard use—that was leaning against one of the trees.

We dispersed. Frank and Molly took the dogs inside to warm up, Ben found something that intrigued him at the back of the house, and Tammy and I headed off to the barn to take care of the horses. It was all idyllic—a beautiful day with good weather, good friends, and good food to come, topped off with that apple crisp.

A half hour later, the horses jumped as Ben came running up, jacket flying open, arms waving, fear trembling in his voice. "Come quick!" he cried. "Aunt Liz has fallen out of the tree and broken her leg."

Ben ran to the house to get his dad while Tammy and I rushed to the front yard where the fruit trees were. There lay Liz, sprawled awkwardly among the apples spilled from her basket. The collapsed ladder lay at her feet. She was composed but obviously in great pain.

"What happened?" I asked.

Between gasps and grimaces, Liz explained that she had just about finished filling her basket when she noticed a few apples on the top branch of the tree. As she stepped onto the fifth rung, the ladder, which was unevenly positioned because of the grade, buckled and dumped her and her apples in a heap. She had landed on her left hip and was certain it was broken.

Before she finished the story, Tammy had pulled out her cell phone and called 911. Ben, Molly, and Frank arrived. The afternoon air had turned chilly, and Frank, ever the gentleman, lay down carefully beside Liz on the ground in an effort to keep her warm. Fortunately the ambulance arrived quickly and took her to the hospital.

X-rays determined that nothing was broken; the pain was the result of pulled tendons and ligaments. We were all relieved and, knowing Liz would be fine in a few weeks, we bundled her up and took her back to the house, where we set her up in a reclining chair and did our best to pamper her. Later that evening, she reminded us of the words in Psalm 68: "Sing to God, sing in praise of his name, extol him who rides on the clouds; rejoice before him—his name is the LORD. A father to the fatherless, a defender of widows, is God in his holy dwelling. God sets the lonely in families" (vv. 4–6).

While on this occasion it was Liz who enjoyed God's provision of friends so close they functioned as a family, I have experienced it too. Deep, time-tested friendships are among the things that allow me to be content being single.

36

Something to Offer

Having friends like Frank, Tammy, Liz, and others who comprise my circle of Christian fellowship has given me perspective. I've been out of the gay life for more than twenty years and am now able to be open about it in ways I wasn't earlier. I'm secure in who I am and don't struggle with either temptation or rejection. When people do learn of my background, they respond in a variety of ways, from discomfort and distance to what sometimes strikes me as an invasive interest. Many have questions, and one of the most important ones is, "What does the church have to offer the struggling homosexual?"

It's important to note the word *struggling*. Many gay men and women are not struggling. They have made peace with their orientation and have found ways of fitting into the broader society either by staying in the closet or owning their preferences and finding acceptance among those who open their hearts to them. However, others do struggle for a variety of reasons. Some yearn for what they see as "normal" social relationships. Others can't accept themselves as they are. Still others want to leave their same-sex attraction behind because of their love for their heterosexual spouse. There are almost as many reasons for struggling as there are people who struggle.

I understand that a growing number of people say that sexual orientation cannot be changed. Be that as it may, what we might call our "personal orientation" *will* change as the Spirit works in us. The Bible makes it clear that the Christian should walk in newness of life, differently from the way we walked in the past, regardless of what that might have been. It is good for all believers to remember that God is in the business of changing us—transforming us "into his image with ever-increasing glory, which comes from the Lord, who is the Spirit" (2 Corinthians 3:18). And we have his promise in this regard: "He who began a good work in you will carry it on to completion until the day of Christ Jesus" (Philippians 1:6).

Few would argue that it is impossible for a liar to become a truth teller, for a thief to become honest, for a hateful person to become loving, for a violent person to become peaceful, for a misogynist to learn to appreciate and value women, and so on. Where there is real desire on the part of a person and supportive people to walk with him or her through the process, we can expect change to happen in the sexual area as well.

Those who have fallen into the trap of objectifying people sexually can learn to look at others as whole persons, not just life-support systems for their sexual organs. The fact that the courts don't label everyone who commits a sexual crime as a dangerous sex offender suggests that society accepts that while some people may be unreformable in their sexual expression (and society needs perpetual protection from them), others are capable of controlling how they act out.

Whether or not a person can be reoriented from homo to hetero or hetero to homo is secondary to the Christian because, quite simply, the Bible makes no specific claims regarding this. What is possible is a reorientation from indiscriminate sexual expression (of *any* kind) to sexual purity. Many men and women at all ages and stages of life choose to live celibate lives for the love of God. No one would claim it is easy, but it is being done by many committed believers even as you are reading this.

All Christians who seek to follow the biblical pattern for sexual expression (within heterosexual, monogamous, lifelong marriage) have the power of the Holy Spirit resident in them to do the will of God regardless of their "natural" tendencies and preferences. I believe all fallen people are oriented toward sin and away from God, regardless of the particular way they manifest it. In Christ, we become new creatures with an orientation away from sin and toward God. While the temptations of the flesh may be strong, I can nevertheless say, based on the authority of the Bible and my own experience, that no temptation we might experience is irresistible (1 Corinthians 10:13).

Operating only in the power of the human will, we are doomed to failure, but through the power of the Holy Spirit we can find both strength for today and hope for tomorrow. There is no substitute for the work of the Holy Spirit in the life of the Christian, regardless of what his or her personal struggle might be.

At the same time, I wouldn't want to suggest that success in the Christian life is solely a partnership between God and an individual. Other Christians play a crucial role of encouragement and support. My own life bears witness to this fact. I couldn't begin to imagine how I would have managed in the early days of transition without the friends who walked with me through my times of frustration and loneliness.

In writing this book, I'm not trying to formulate policy or offer a method of any kind. I'm simply telling my own story and putting it on the record. No one pressured me to leave my gay life behind. I simply came to the point where I wanted healthy, loving relationships more than I wanted sex. I wanted what I hadn't had during my twenty years in the gay scene. Every relationship I had then had sexual overtones. I constantly evaluated other guys and situations that could lead to a sexual encounter of some kind, and frankly, every instance I could imagine had the potential to end in a sexual experience. That's where I was, and when I'd had my fill of it, I was ready to submit to God's work in my life.

I believe that when a gay person is exposed to the truth of God presented in an appropriately loving way, and when he (or she) truly understands it and embraces it, he will want to experience the inner change God wants to effect in his life because it will bring him closer to the God who made him, loves him, and died for him.

One thing the church needs to accept is that sexual sins, of whatever kind, are not worse than other sins. We need to learn to extend grace to people who are in process. If an alcoholic received the truth and began the process of drying out and abandoning his reliance on alcohol, the church would rally around. If, after some weeks of sobriety, he went on a bender, his Christian friends would not throw him on the scrap heap as a failure. They would pick him up, dust him off, and walk forward with him. We need to do the same thing with sexual sinners.

If the church thinks that people can attain a level of perfection instantaneously, then the church falls short in understanding the human condition as spelled out in the Bible. Even people who are cooperating with God in developing a healthy sexual perspective and practice may slip occasionally. Some don't, but some do. The lingering influence of a Victorian attitude toward sex leads us to be harsh with such slips. God is serious about how serious stepping out of his plan for sexual expression is, but he is also serious about proud hearts, gossiping tongues, and unforgiving spirits.

As long as the struggler confesses his sin to God and to those he has hurt and purposes to move on, he is on the right track and needs the embrace of his fellow Christians. This is true for all of us, because all of us are in exactly this position. Yet often I don't see the church extend the same grace to sexual sinners that it extends to almost every other kind of offender.

We are called to show Christ's love. He knew the weaknesses of his disciples, their slowness to understand, and their stumbling faith, yet he kept working with them anyway. Given our own tendency to fail, especially in self-righteous ways, we need to raise the bar for ourselves and drop it for others. We need to speak the truth, but always in love. As Paul said to the Christians in Galatia, "If someone is caught in a sin, you who live by the Spirit should restore that person gently. But watch yourselves, or you also may be tempted" (Galatians 6:1). Restoration is a process, and while some people make amazingly rapid progress, others are slower. We need to work with people through the process at whatever pace they go and not abandon them when we decide they've used up their chances. That is a human construct. As long as people keep repenting, God keeps forgiving.

Expressions of care and love are crucial. Will the whole church accept this? Probably not. But perhaps some individual Christians can receive it and start building into the lives of people who are struggling with homosexuality, promiscuity, sex addiction, and other sexual issues. When we begin to understand church fellowship as parallel to biblical marriage, we'll remain committed to each other—in bad times as well as good times.

37

The Last Word

Is there a price to pay for missing God's standard or rebelling? At some level, there always is, though sometimes his mercy is so great that the price is nowhere close to what it might be. In this age of grace, he doesn't treat us according to our sin.

I know I've lost things I'll never get back. I lost what I had with Audrey and years of being a father to Sean. I separated myself from good and faithful friends who would have built positively into my life. I not only missed many opportunities to honor God with my life, but I actively brought reproach on his name. I regret these things now as I recognize what I lost for short-term gain, if I can call it that.

At the same time, God's grace has been evident in powerful ways. Though I repeatedly placed myself in harm's way through unprotected sexual experiences, I never got HIV/AIDS. Despite years of drug use, I never got caught, so I have no criminal record and no long-term ill effects from this activity.

While my life has not unfolded as I now wish it had, I'm happy with it as it is—with friends, with my son, Sean, and with Audrey and her husband. I believe the way things are now is the best they can be, given the many selfish choices I made in the past.

Mostly, I'm happy to be back on track spiritually. My relationship with God means more to me than anything else, and though I walked away from him for twenty years, he never abandoned me. He was at work behind the scenes all that time, protecting me from my own bad decisions while allowing me to exhaust myself in the pursuit of the pleasure of sin for that season. Then he graciously drew me back into fellowship with himself and his people so I could honestly say that this part of my life was over, and I was out.

Some of my readers may be curious about the current status of my family relationships. This prompts me to outline them in a general way. I am grateful for the positive changes I've seen.

Gwen

From the time we were older teens, Gwen had always been accepting of me. We've had the closest of all of my sibling relationships. She was the family spokesperson, reassuring me that though I had chosen to pursue same-sex relationships, I was still accepted. We still have a congenial relationship, though my pursuit of the things of the Lord has turned out to be more of an obstacle than my associating with the gay community.

Our lives are very different, but I can be open and honest with her when we talk. No hidden agendas or unspoken expectations get in the way. We don't merely relate as brother and sister—we really like each other, which is a wonderful thing between siblings. Also, Gwen's husband, Tony, is a great fellow, and I get along well with him, which makes my relationship with the two of them rich and rewarding.

Barb

My sister Barb has had a difficult life. Her husband pursued a relationship with someone else, leaving her to raise their two sons, both of whom have autism spectrum disorder, one more severely than the other.

Barb has leaned hard on her church friends, who have been a great support to her.

On a couple of occasions I surprised her by showing up at her church to sit with her during the service and then take her out afterward. She was delighted by these special occasions, and I liked seeing her happiness. These visits gave me the opportunity to meet some of her friends and be a little more connected with her life.

Now she has developed symptoms of Alzheimer's disease, which has made things more complicated, but she still enjoys moments of clarity.

Yvonne

Yvonne was the most cheerful one in our family and remained so right up to the end of her life. I visited her a couple of days before she died, and the nurse kindly delayed her morphine injection so she could respond. The Lord gave us some lovely time when she was lucid and without pain, and we were able to have a great conversation in the company of some other family members and friends. We talked about her going home to heaven, and she smiled warmly. Her verbal abilities were all but gone, but the peace of God shone on her face. It was a great opportunity to connect with her one last time.

Ken

Ken was my absentee big brother for most of my life, but recently we've been able to pick up the pieces and reconnect in a meaningful way. We have a growing, positive relationship and have been able to stay in close touch by phone, email, and occasional visits. His daughters and their families have included me in milestone events, and I've thrown Ken regular birthday parties since his eightieth. That has given us a great chance to be together as a family at my place. This has deepened my bond with Ken, his wife, and their children. It's been great to see a softening and gentleness developing in his personality. I feel that the Lord has restored the years that the locusts had eaten in regard to our relationship.

Sean

Sean has been a bit of a puzzle in my life with his comings and goings, though there is no doubt God used him to make a significant impact on me. Sean has been involved with a small sect in Western Canada for several years now. His time with me ebbed and flowed according to his relationship with the group. At one point he moved back to Ontario and worked with me for several months before returning to Alberta. Later he came back and again lived with me briefly before moving to another Ontario town for a while and then returning to Alberta for another stint. When he has been in Ontario, we have worked together and enjoyed our father-son relationship, though we are in different places spiritually.

I reach out to him in what are meaningful ways to me. Lately those gestures have been reciprocated with a depth and sincerity I appreciate. We're keeping in touch now by email and phone. I sense a growing warmth and bond with Sean and hope it will continue.

Audrey

My relationship with Audrey since Sean and I reconnected has been good. We're in touch with each other from time to time. She has had her challenges. The man she married after we were divorced passed away, and she spent some time as a widow until she remarried. During one of the occasions when Sean was in Ontario, she came to visit us and, for more than a week, spent time with Sean and me each day, often having our evening meal together. Far from awkward, it was actually very pleasant. Later, some of the "if only" thoughts arose, but we accepted that some things from the past can't be undone. She has meaningful work in Scripture translation and is happy and fulfilled. She lives with her husband in Florida now, and I'm happy for her.

Current Friendships

My closest circle of friends is drawn from my fellow Christians who form Believers' Bible Fellowship. Several of these were among the first friends I made at Greenwood Gospel Chapel. They have continued to provide me with the impetus to grow, not only spiritually but also socially and emotionally. My relationships with them are mature and secure. I have the utmost confidence in my brothers and sisters and sense that they trust me in a way that has contributed strongly to the process of building healthy perceptions of myself and others. Together we encourage each other to maximize our spiritual gifts as we serve each other and the community in various ways. I can't say strongly enough how the lasting impact of these relationships has blessed me as I have taken my place in the family of God.

The quietness and solitude provided by my country setting allow me to relish my relationship with the Lord. My mornings are exceptionally special. When I first moved in, a friend expressed concern that I would be lonely, but I don't think I've experienced five minutes of loneliness in all the time I've been there. The Lord is truly sufficient.

The place is way too big for me. It's too much work for me. It's a whole lot more than I require, but it's what the Lord has given me at this time. It's wonderful to be able to share it with my friends. I don't have specific plans regarding it for the future, but I hope the Lord will use it to bless more and more people. It's a special, special place.

When friends come, we work together, do projects together, play games together, and have fellowship together. Their children are like grandchildren to me. Those who are old enough drive the tractor and cut grass. The younger ones love to help as best they can but often end up playing with the horses, dogs, and cat.

When I'm away, people are always ready to move in to watch the place for me. They bring their children or grandchildren and treat my home as their own. I cherish these friendships and the way we build into each other's lives in practical as well as spiritual ways.

Because of the space the Lord has given me, I've been able to host some larger events. On one occasion a group of sixty immigrants and refugees who were participating in an ESL program spent an afternoon walking in the forest, riding the horses, and watching the hens in the chicken coop. These were new experiences for many of them, and I felt privileged that I could give them the opportunity.

My current friendships are so much more real than the relationships I had in the past. There's no hidden agenda or purpose in the friendships I have now. They are more wholesome, meaningful, and consequently more powerful in my life. I enjoy being able to sit with a group of friends, whether few or many, and not be preoccupied with who I might be spending the night with or wondering who is finding me attractive enough to pair off with. So much of my social life in the past was seriously misguided. What I have now is completely different.

Looking back, I see that my relationships in the old days were all about taking. Even if we were engaged in something like sports, a business arrangement, or even fund-raising for some gay cause, I was always on the hunt for some personal, usually sexual, benefit (and I want to say I'm speaking only for myself here). Now when I look at people, I see them through God's eyes as well as my own. I see their value as people with whom I can work to meet needs in the community, not just my own needs. Above all, I seek to glorify God together with them.

Now the question in mind when I have visitors to the farm is, "How can I minister to these folks?" Sometimes, when I'm working with people who have bigger challenges, I invite some of my church friends to come and help me. There is community. There is teamwork. There is shared purpose. Talk about a change in orientation—this has been huge!

Acknowledgments

I thank God for the grace and love extended to me, and for the restoration and victory that only he can give.

I thank my family and friends for all the support and encouragement I received in the process of telling my story.

I owe a special thanks to Ron Hughes who articulated and patiently walked me through my journey.

And I thank all the staff at Kregel Publications for making it happen.